Boulder County, Colorado District Court Judge's Docket, Volume 1

1867-1872

An Annotated Index

Compiled by Dina C. Carson

Boulder County, Colorado District Court Judge's Docket, Volume 1,

1867-1872

An Annotated Index

Compiled by Dina C. Carson

Published by:

Iron Gate Publishing
P.O. Box 999
Niwot, CO 80544
www.irongate.com

Copyright © 2016 by Dina C. Carson, Iron Gate Publishing

Printed in the United States of America

ISBN   1-68224-026-6   ISBN 13   978-1-68224-026-7

Introduction

Boulder did not have a courthouse until 1867 and many of the cases that occurred before that time were sent to Golden in Jefferson County or Denver in Arapahoe County. After the courthouse was built, many of those cases were returned to Boulder. The *Boulder County, Colorado District Court Judge's Docket, Volume 1, 1867-1872* contains the plaintiffs and defendants, often lists which attorneys represented which side in the case, gives the docket number in the Grand Docket (once that numbering system began), and has the judge's notes for how the case proceeded or the verdict, where appropriate.

The Docket contains three types of cases: Criminal, Civil (referred to in this volume as Law cases) and Chancery.

The original book contains a page numbering irregularity: page 319 follows 262, page 318 follows 319, and page 263 resumes after 318.

The first section of this book has a list of cases in the order that they first appear. The earliest cases do not have grand docket (GD) numbers. After the initial list of cases, the cases appear in order of the grand docket number. Not every possible grand docket number appears in the original book.

The second section of this book has the index of participants and their roles in each case.

Legal terms found in this volume:
> Appellant—A person who appeals a case to a higher court.
> Appellee—A person who responds to a case appealed to a higher court.
> Assumpsit—An action to recover damages for breach of a contract.
> Attachment— Seizing property in anticipation of a favorable ruling for a plaintiff who claims to be owed money by the defendant.
> Foreclosure—A lender claims possession of property belonging to a borrower, who has stopped making payments to the lender.
> Mechanics Lien— A guarantee of payment to builders, contracters and construction firms that build or repair structures.
> Replevin— A legal action taken to reclaim goods which have been wrongfully taken, detained or distrained.
> Trespass— To infringe upon a property owner's legal right to enjoy the benefits of ownership.

The original *Boulder County, Colorado District Court Judge's Docket, Volume 1, 1867-1872* is held by the Colorado State Archives and is accessible for research. You can order a copies of pages from this ledger by calling the Colorado State Archives, or placing an order through their website.

The People of the Territory of Colorado vs Charles Knopple

The People of the Territory of Colorado vs Jessie [Jesse] Harris

The People of the Territory of Colorado vs John C Carter

The People of the Territory of Colorado vs Samuel L Noblet [Noblit]

John Cook vs Sealy [Selah] F Roberts, et al

Henry Welman [Wellman] et al vs Samuel Hayden

David Parlin vs Peter M Housel and John DeBacker

Columbus Weese vs John C Carter

Harrison Goodwin vs Henry Richart and Jacob Bruce

John M Hewes vs Cary Culver

Niwot & Black Hawk Wagon Road Co vs Eric Chapman

Niwot & Black Hawk Wagon Road Co vs Frederick Affolter

Niwot & Black Hawk Wagon Road Co vs George C Beckwith

Niwot & Black Hawk Wagon Road Co vs Isaac Richardson

Niwot & Black Hawk Wagon Road Co vs George W Chambers

Healey & Holt vs Samuel Copeland

Healey & Holt vs Tourtellot & Squires

Richard Sopris vs Boulder County

S H Carr and J B Holingsworth vs E J Coffman

Niwot Mining Company vs John Barter et al

Andrew J Maxwell vs Samuel Akins

D C Maxon vs D L Miller and James B Foote

Albert G Soule vs Stephen H Green

Jonathan Linclow vs Joseph F Gile

Daniel Delahunt vs Patrick Shanahan et al

James A Brown and Francis E Brown vs Henry A Buttles

William McDunn vs Charles Donald et al

E M Rhodes vs Edward Froggett

Amos Widner vs James A Carr

Calvin W Ward vs James A Carr

William D Pennock vs Elijah H Andrews

William Gafton vs Amander Barker

Thomas J Jones vs Peter M Housel & John DeBacker

Joseph M Marshall vs William Morgan et al

Edward Froggett vs Jane Froggett

Mary Ferguson vs Moses Ferguson

Andrew J Mackey [Macky] vs Charles P Hamblin et al

Elias Bailey vs Selsana & W H Gould

The People of the Territory of Colorado vs Warren Patter

The People of the Territory of Colorado vs Junius Berkley and William H Smith

The People of the Territory of Colorado vs Daniel Moore

Jeremiah W Whipple vs Austin Smith

The People of the Territory of Colorado vs J Carrie White

The People of the Territory of Colorado vs James Parker

The People of the Territory of Colorado vs Geo C Squires

The People of the Territory of Colorado vs William B Westlake

The People of the Territory of Colorado vs Manning S Harmon

The People of the Territory of Colorado vs John Solander

The People of the Territory of Colorado vs Calvin Bard

[Some of the cases above will appear again with docket numbers].

[In the cases below, a few cases are listed using the same grand docket number].

GD 1   The People of the Territory of Colorado vs Charles Knopple

GD 2   The People of the Territory of Colorado vs Jesse Harris

GD 6   Henry Welman [Wellman] et al vs Samuel Hayden

GD 9   Harrison Goodwin vs Henry Richart & Jacob Bruce

GD 11   Edward Froggett vs Jane Froggett

GD 13	Andrew J Macky vs Charles Hamblin & Calvin W Ward
GD 14	John M Hewes vs Cary Culver
GD 27	D C Maxon vs D L Miller and James B Foote
GD 29	Jotham/Jonathan Linclaw/Linclow vs Joseph Gile
GD 30	Daniel Delahunt vs Patrick Shanahan et al
GD 31	James A Brown & Frances E Brown vs Henry A Buttles
GD 32	William McDunn vs Charles Donald et al
GD 35	William Grafton vs Amander Barker
GD 36	Amos Widner vs James A Carr
GD 38	William D Pennock vs Elijah H Andrews
GD 39	Thomas J Jones vs Peter M Housel & John DeBacker
GD 40	The People of the Territory of Colorado vs Alfred Cushman
GD 41	The People of the Territory of Colorado vs Samuel Berger and Leroy Cole
GD 42	The People of the Territory of Colorado vs Charles Lockridge
GD 43	The People of the Territory of Colorado vs Alfred Cushman
GD 44	The People of the Territory of Colorado vs James E Dubois & William Dubois
GD 45	The People of the Territory of Colorado vs Joseph Springall, Charles Bishop and Walter Heredge
GD 46	James M Campbell vs Samuel Cushman, Levi Cressey, dba Cushman & Cressey
GD 47	Harrison Goodwin vs Henry Richart & Jacob Bruce, et al
GD 48	Jasper Sears vs Stephen Phillips
GD 49	S M Blair vs George Zweck
GD 51	Julius Jincks vs Jacob M Hickes & William W Haus
GD 52	Jesse M Sherwood vs Nephi M Howard
GD 52	Chester M Cole vs James M Smith
GD 53	Anthony Arnett vs Joseph Springall
GD 53	Chester M Cole vs James M Smith
GD 54	Francis Rink vs Fletcher Earnest

GD 55   Daniel Meginnes vs L B Jackson & D A Springer

GD 57   George McGowen vs Amos Bixley

GD 58   Sally Lackman vs Andrew Douty & Sylvester Douty

GD 59   Joseph Cofield vs Edward Dunstan & Thomas Dunston

GD 60   George D Cook vs Samuel Cushman, Levi Cressey, Amasa G
Bixby, Amos Bixby, Jonathan Lin, dba Cushman & Cressey

GD 61   Henry Bell vs Elijah Lovejoy

GD 62   David Hoyt vs Charles Campbell & George W Chambers

GD 64   Jasper Sears vs Stephen Phillips

GD 67   The People of the Territory of Colorado vs Daniel Moore

GD 67   The People of Colorado Territory vs John Hollingsworth

GD 68   William E Darby vs Arthur G Raynor

GD 69   Thomas Morros vs Frank Bacon, John Richardson, Archibald
Stewart, William H Davidson

GD 70   Hiram Harmon vs Jacob Hickes

GD 71   Alfred H Clements vs Jacob M Sullivan, David W Nichols,
Luther C Wellman, Sylvanus Weljman, C P Cluff

GD 72   William McDunn vs Isaac A Gardener & John J Wallace

GD 74   Charles C Lawson vs Joseph Milner, Jr

GD 75   Charles Terry & John Terry vs Anthony Arnett

GD 76   Charles Terry & John O Terry vs Erick J Anderson

GD 77   E D Crawford vs J M Hickes

GD 78   John M Hulling vs Henry Green et al

GD 79   James Carroll vs Henry Green et al

GD 80   John Collier vs Henry Green et al

GD 81   Thomas J Oyler, Henry Neikirk & Clarence P Elder vs Alpheus
Wright

GD 82   Thomas J Oyler, Henry Neikirk & Clarence P Elder vs Alpheus
Wright

GD 83   Samuel Copeland vs George W Nichols

GD 84   The People of Colorado vs John M Hulling et al

GD 85	The People of the Territory of Colorado vs Lafayette Akins
GD 86	The People of the Territory of Colorado vs John Hollingworth
GD 87	Granville Berkley vs E H Andrews
GD 88	Gottlieb Bestle vs Abraham Gifford
GD 89	Lucy B Partridge vs Erick J Anderson
GD 90	William Pound, Adm of D Pound estate vs William Wain & Elizabeth Wain
GD 91	John M Hewes vs Samuel Copeland
GD 92	William A H Loveland, Samuel Copeland, dba Loveland & Copeland vs John M Hewes
GD 93	Albion B Daniels, J Sidney Brown, dba Daniels & Brown vs John M Hewes
GD 94	Albion B Daniels, J Sidney Brown, dba Daniels & Brown vs Frederick C Beckwith & Lawson Beckwith
GD 95	Henry Neikirk vs Henry Green et al
GD 96	George W Jackson vs Henry Green et al
GD 97	John Shourds vs Henry Green et al
GD 98	Thomas Tumbleson vs Henry Green et al
GD 98	John Hesler vs Henry Green et al
GD 99	John Hesler vs Henry Green et al
GD 100	William C Stone vs Henry Green et al
GD 101	Lewis D Dougherty vs Henry Green et al
GD 102	A E Lea vs Henry Green et al
GD 103	Andrew J Slack vs Henry Green et al
GD 104	David Evans vs Henry Green et al
GD 105	A B Judson vs John M Veasey
GD 105	Isaac Sherman vs Cilenda Sherman
GD 106	Abbie F Pease vs Charles F Pease
GD 108	The People of the Territory of Colorado vs Charles Geer, James Bristol & James Simpson

GD 109	The People of the Territory of Colorado vs Solomon Geer & Loyd Streaver
GD 110	The People of the Territory of Colorado vs Thomas Lamelson
GD 110	The People of the Territory of Colorado vs Jesse Harris
GD 111	Anna Waeneke vs Adolf Waeneke
GD 112	John H Terry vs Hugh Wedge
GD 113	Albion B Daniels, J Sidney Brown, dba Daniels & Brown (appellee) vs Lawson Beckwith (appellant)
GD 114	Charles A Stewart (appellant) vs William H Fry (appellee)
GD 115	Daniel Sayre vs William E Darley
GD 115	The People of the Territory of Colorado vs Edward P Kinney
GD 116	Mary Jane Jay vs Orson Jay
GD 117	The People of Colorado Territory vs Hugh Owens
GD 118	The People of the Territory of Colorado on behalf of James W Partridge, Sidney B Morrison, dba Partridge & Morrison vs Henry Green, Marinus G Smith, Anthony Arnett & Frederick W Kohler
GD 119	George W Hold & George W Baker vs Samuel F Reynolds, Wm Y Todd, J D Scott & Geo W Chambers
GD 120	Robert Culver (appellant) vs Wilhelm Sommers (appellee)
GD 121	Margrett Pell vs James M Pell
GD 122	Anthony Arnett vs Robert Harman
GD 123	The People of Colorado Territory vs James B Savits
GD 124	Joseph Williams (appellee) vs Edward P Kinney (appellant)
GD 125	Michael Mooney vs Niwot Mining Company
GD 126	Robert Ellingham, John Ellingham, dba Ellingham Brothers vs Niwot Mining Company
GD 126	Michael Mooney vs Niwot Mining Company
GD 127	Anthony Arnett (appellant) vs Edward P Kinney & Clarissa P Kinney (appellee)
GD 128	Hanson Snyder, Richard Elems vs Niwot Mining Company

GD 129   George H Church vs Alonzo Allen

GD 130   George H Church vs Alonzo Wilson

GD 131   Anna W Taft vs Benj A Taft

GD 132   William Pound vs Frances M Smith & James M Smith

GD 133   Charles Dabney vs Thomas J Graham

GD 134   Roger S Lowe vs Mathilda S M Pound, Ephraim Pound, William Pound, Joseph Pound, Mary A Frost, Immagene Pound, Isabella B Pound, Byron Pound, Elias S Pound, Charlie Pound, Millie Pouns & Eugene Morrill

GD 135   Patrick Hannah vs Thomas Conoy

GD 136   Peter Powell vs John C Carter

GD 137   The People of the Territory of Colorado for the use of Warren Hussey & Frank Palmer, dba Warren Hussey & Company vs William H Dickens & Harvey Manners

GD 138   Austin Smith vs Decater Farrar & William W Coulson

GD 139   Joseph E Bates vs Jotham Gould

GD 140   Henry Mathis vs Erin Mathis

GD 141   Charles L Wood vs Royal Jacobs & Horatio Jacobs

GD 142   John Lickes vs Frank Shores

GD 143   John Duncan vs Erick J Anderson, Under Sheriff & Henry Green, Sheriff

GD 144   Braton Maury vs Junius E Wharton

GD 145   Samuel T Noblit (appellant) vs Granville Berkley (appellee)

GD 146   Joseph M Shelton vs Erick J Anderson

GD 147   Charles C Johnson vs Alpheus Wright

GD 148   The People of the Territory of Colorado on behalf of James W Partridge, Sidney B Morrison, dba Partridge & Morrison vs Henry Green, Marinus G Smith, Anthony Arnett & Frederick W Kohler

GD 149   James A Maxwell vs William A Corson & Almenia A Allen

GD 150   Cornelius Guilfoyle vs Niwot Mining Company

GD 151   Niwot & Black Hawk Wagon Road Company (appellee) vs William Davidson (appellant)

GD 152   Thomas Mathews, William Trevan, Thomas Terrill & Thomas Boase vs Niwot Mining Company

GD 153   Margret E Cadey vs Elisha N Haney

GD 154   The People of the Territory of Colorado vs Edward P Kinney

GD 156   The People of the Territory of Colorado vs Edward Donnelly

GD 158   William S Chamberlain vs Thomas Scott

GD 158   Lucinda Towner vs Reuben Towner

GD 159   Anthony Arnett vs John Harris & Benj Harris

GD 160   Andrew J Macky, Frederick A Squires & James V Pomeroy vs Junius E Wharton

GD 161   Edward Donnelly vs John P Harris

GD 162   Augustus R Stewart vs John P Harris

GD 163   Manning S Harman vs John P Harris

GD 164   Stafford J Pratt vs James W Johnson

GD 165   Jonathan A Tourtellot, Frederick A Squires, dba Tourtellot & Squires vs Alpheus Wright, Augustine B Crosby, Jerome Thomas & John Wetherbee

GD 166   Joseph B Williams (appellee) vs Edward P Kinney (appellant)

GD 167   Charles W Smart vs Junius E Wharton

GD 168   Hercules Graham (appellant) vs William Bryant (appellee)

GD 170   William Bryant vs Alpheus Wright, John Wetherbee & Lyman Cook, dba A Wright & Company

GD 171   Henry O Wells vs Alpheus Wright, John Wetherbee & Lyman Cook, dba A Wright & Company

GD 172   Henry O Wells vs Alpheus Wright, John Wetherbee & Lyman Cook, dba A Wright & Company

GD 173   Gardner P Wood vs Alpheus Wright, John Wetherbee & Lyman Cook, dba A Wright & Company

GD 174   Gardner P Wood vs Alpheus Wright, John Wetherbee & Lyman Cook, dba A Wright & Company

GD 175	Jesse F Allum vs Alpheus Wright, John Wetherbee & Lyman Cook, dba A Wright & Company
GD 176	Jesse F Allum vs Alpheus Wright, John Wetherbee & Lyman Cook, dba A Wright & Company
GD 177	Daniel H Cressman vs Alpheus Wright, John Wetherbee & Lyman Cook, dba A Wright & Company
GD 178	Daniel H Cressman vs Alpheus Wright, John Wetherbee & Lyman Cook, dba A Wright & Company
GD 179	Samuel Wills vs Samuel Hayden
GD 180	Samuel Copeland & W A H Loveland, dba Loveland & Copeland (appellee) vs Amos Widner (appellant)
GD 181	Granville Berkley vs Horace A Wolcott & George F Chase
GD 182	Horace A Wolcott vs William H Osborn & Daniel O Osborn
GD 183	John Jones vs John M Hewes & Anthony Arnett
GD 184	William B Fowler vs Alpheus Wright, Augustine B Crosby, Chas H Crosby, John Wetherbee, Lyman A Cook, Jerome Thomas, George Merrill, dba A Wright & Company and Charles C Welch, William R Horton, C B Snider and John W Besler
GD 185	Edward Donnelly vs John C Bailey
GD 186	The People of the Territory of Colorado vs James Parker
GD 187	The People of the Territory of Colorado vs James Parker
GD 188	The People of the Territory of Colorado vs James Parker
GD 189	The People of the Territory of Colorado vs J Carrie White
GD 190	The People of the Territory of Colorado vs J Carrie White
GD 191	The People of the Territory of Colorado vs Carrie White
GD 194	The People of the Territory of Colorado vs Wm B Westlake
GD 196	The People of the Territory of Colorado vs John Rothrick [Rothrock]
GD 197	The People of the Territory of Colorado vs Charles H Hook
GD 198	The People of the Territory of Colorado vs Charles H Hook
GD 199	The People of the Territory of Colorado vs John Rothrick [Rothrock]

GD 201	Frederick A Squires, Jonathan Tourtellot, dba Tourtellot & Squires vs Alpheus Wright, Augustine B Crosby, John Wetherbee, Lyman Cook, dba A Wright & Company
GD 202	Luther C Wellman, Sylvanus Wellman vs Alpheus Wright, John Wetherbee, Lyman Cook, Aubustine B Crosby, dba A Wright & Company
GD 203	Anthony Arnett vs Alpheus Wright, Augustine B Crosby, Charles H Crosby, Lyman A Cook, John Wetherbee, George W Morrill & Jerome Thomas, dba A Wright & Company
GD 204	John W Smith vs Decatur Farrar
GD 205	Jonas Anderson (appellee) vs Roger S Lowe (appellant)
GD 206	Charles W Johnson (appellant) vs James Doran (appellee)
GD 207	Perry White vs James Morrison
GD 208	The People of the Territory of Colorado vs Martin Leyden
GD 210	John W Smith vs Austin Smith
GD 211	John W Smith vs Wm W Coulson, Harriet D Smith, Clarissa A Coulson
GD 212	Granville Berkley, Thomas J Graham & Frederick C Beckwith vs John Virden, George W Webster, George F Chase, Robert J Woodward, Jas H Decker, David H Nichols, C P Cluff, Luther C Wellman, Jacob M Sullivan & Wellman & Sullivan
GD 213	Anthony Arnett vs Alexander Safely
GD 214	Jesse M Sherwood vs Nephi M Howard, Norman R Howard
GD 215	Henry L Carter vs Amander Barker
GD 216	Barnabus B Anthor vs John M Ware, Granville Berkley & William B Alford
GD 217	William A Corson (appellee) vs Wm L Hopkins (appellant)
GD 218	Jason L Dwight vs William Finch and Joseph Davis, dba Finch & Davis
GD 219	John F McGahey vs William Finch and Joseph Davis, dba Finch & Davis
GD 220	Elias Gouldman, Gustatus Fall & Arnold Fall (appellee) vs Jacob Altmark (appellant)

GD 221	John W Goss (appellant) vs Charles Allman (appellee)
GD 222	Charles A Stewart (appellee) vs Elijah H Andrews (appellant)
GD 223	Jemima Maddox vs Peter Maddox
GD 224	Charles F Calwell vs E M Bard
GD 225	William A Davidson (appellee) vs Andrew J Kimber (appellant)
GD 226	Martin B Hayes vs Consolidated Gregory Company
GD 227	Noble Wade vs James A Maxwell, James P Maxwell, James T Maddox, and W D Polly
GD 228	Rocky Mountain National Bank vs Union Gold Mining Company of Colorado
GD 229	The People of the Territory of Colorado vs A G Burk
GD 230	Granville Berkley vs James Safely
GD 231	Thomas J Richman vs The Consolidated Gregory Company
GD 232	The New York Gold Mining Company vs Consolidated Gregory Company
GD 233	James S Kelsey vs Oren H Henry & Ormal E Henry
GD 234	Rufus Clapp vs Joseph Francis
GD 235	The People of the Territory of Colorado vs John Wilson
GD 236	The People of the Territory of Colorado vs John Wilson
GD 237	The People of the Territory of Colorado vs Calvin Bard
GD 238	The People of the Territory of Colorado vs Calvin Bard
GD 240	The People of the Territory of Colorado vs John Miller
GD 241	The People of the Territory of Colorado vs William F Sears, Peter Werley
GD 242	The People of the Territory of Colorado vs Frederick Brandey
GD 243	The People of the Territory of Colorado vs Giles H Fonda
GD 244	The People of the Territory of Colorado vs Harrison F Orvis
GD 245	The People of the Territory of Colorado vs John Thompson
GD 246	The People of the Territory of Colorado vs Leo Donnelly
GD 247	The People of the Territory of Colorado vs William B Westlake
GD 248	The People of the Territory of Colorado vs James Parker

GD 249	The People of the Territory of Colorado vs William Johnson
GD 250	Thomas Scott vs William S Chamberlain & Robert Culver
GD 253	The People of the Territory of Colorado vs Hiram E Washburn
GD 254	Charles C Lawson (appellee) vs Joseph Sheldon (appellant)
GD 255	Lucinda Towner vs Reuben Towner
GD 256	Mary E Fowler vs Henry Fowler
GD 257	Jeremiah W Whipple vs Elizabeth A Whipple
GD 258	Joseph A Griswold, Henry F Griswold & Francis A Sanford, dba J A & H F Griswold vs George L Beckwith, Oscar F Beckwith & James M Smith, dba Smith & Beckwith
GD 259	George W Chamberlain vs George L Beckwith, Isaac Richardson, Lawson Beckwith & E W Chapman
GD 260	Manerva Jane Slater vs William C Slater
GD 261	Samuel E Brown vs E N Beach
GD 262	Elias S Stewart vs Nathan W Brown
GD 263	Charles A Trowbridge vs William A Davidson
GD 264	Elias S Stewart vs Nathan W Brown
GD 265	William W Baldwin vs John W Ritchie
GD 266	Charles A Trowbridge vs William A Davidson
GD 267	Charles Dabney vs Thomas J Graham
GD 268	Dyre N Garner & Lyman A White vs William J Mann
GD 269	James Parker (appellee) vs John DeBacker, Carl Blake & Herman Seman (appellants)
GD 270	The People of the Territory of Colorado vs Reuben Towner
GD 271	The People of the Territory of Colorado vs John DeBacker
GD 272	John W Thomas vs Johnathan J Cranmer
GD 272	Willard Teller vs Board of County Commissioners of Boulder County
GD 273	Willard Teller vs Board of County Commissioners of Boulder County
GD 274	The People of the Territory of Colorado vs A D Bruster

GD 275	D G Scouten (appellee) vs Henry W Cort (appellant)
GD 277	The People of the Territory of Colorado vs John B Finch
GD 277	The People of the Territory of Colorado vs John B Ford
GD 278	The People of the Territory of Colorado vs Charles E Baker/ Barber
GD 279	The People of the Territory of Colorado vs Nathan W Brown
GD 280	A N Allen (appellee) vs Louise P Beckwith (appellant)
GD 281	Stephen Bailey vs A R Day
GD 282	Daniel B Jones (appellee) vs Samuel Graham (appellant)
GD 283	Calvin J Mosher vs Ellen Mosher
GD 285	Daniel Witter & Court C Clements vs Henry Clements
GD 286	Sarah Spurlock vs George N Spurlock
GD 288	David G Peabody vs George W hambers & Samuel M Hays
GD 289	Andrew J Macky vs Jerome Thomas
GD 290	Andrew J Macky vs Jerome Thomas & Alpheus Wright
GD 291	Charles A Trowbridge vs Hanson Snyder, Richard Elems, Robert Ellingham, John Ellingham, Michael Mooney, Cornelius Guilfoyle, Jonathan S Smith, William A Davidson
GD 292	Matilda Parlin vs Andrew Pedee
GD 293	Board of County Commissioners of Boulder for the use of Abner R Brown Superintendant of Schools of Boulder County vs Alanson R Day, Charles Dabney, A J Macky, James Parker & Ephraim Pound
GD 294	Michael Cocoman (appellee) vs William H Rice (appellant)
GD 295	Anna Perdue vs Alison B Perdue
GD 296	Maria Tourtellot vs James V Pomeroy & Ormel E Henry, dba Pomeroy & Henry
GD 297	Anthony Arnett vs Samuel F Rannells, Benjamin B Rannells & William N Rannells, dba S F Rannals & Son
GD 298	Jackson J Dunagan vs Nathan W Brown
GD 299	James Clark vs J J Cranmer

GD 300   Thomas Orchard, John Orchard & William W Ramage, dba London and Colorado Company vs Charles Callender, Theodore E Perkins, William H Stowe & Charles R Richardson, dba Richardson, Stowe & Company

GD 301   Mathew D Brett vs Charles M Coulson, Charles Emerson & Walter A Buckingham

GD 301   Reuben E Towner vs Oscar Allen & Mansfield Towner

GD 301   P M Hinman (appellee) vs Amos Widner (appellant)

GD 302   Samuel Graham & John Davis vs Charles S Richardson, Charles Callender, Milton Stowe, harles E Perkins, dba Richardson, Stowe & Company and Thomas Orchard, John Orchard, dba London and Colorado Company

GD 304   The People of the Territory of Colorado vs John Williams

GD 305   Boulder Valley Railroad and Telegraph Extention Company

GD 306   Denver and Boulder Valley Railway and Telegraph Extention Company vs Matilda Parlin

GD 307   The People of the Territory of Colorado vs John McMahan

GD 308   The People of the Territory of Colorado vs Mary Solander

A

A Wright & Company
defendant; 1870 Jan; pg 153; GD 169; Law; mechanics lien
defendant; 1870 Jan; pg 154; GD 171; Law; mechanics lien
defendant; 1870 Jan; pg 154; [GD 170]; Law; attachment
defendant; 1870 Jan; pg 155; GD 173; Law; attachment
defendant; 1870 Jan; pg 155; GD 172; Law; attachment
defendant; 1870 Jan; pg 156; GD 175; Law; mechanics lien
defendant; 1870 Jan; pg 156; GD 174; Law; mechanics lien
defendant; 1870 Jan; pg 157; GD 177; Law; mechanics lien
defendant; 1870 Jan; pg 157; GD 176; Law; attachment
defendant; 1870 Jan; pg 158; GD 178; Law; attachment
defendant; 1870 Jan; pg 161; GD 184; Law; mechanics lien
defendant; 1871 Jan; pg 182; GD 170; Law; attachment
defendant; 1871 Jan; pg 182; GD 169; Law; mechanics lien
defendant; 1871 Jan; pg 183; GD 171; Law; mechanics lien
defendant; 1871 Jan; pg 183; GD 172; Law; attachment
defendant; 1871 Jan; pg 184; GD 173; Law; attachment
defendant; 1871 Jan; pg 184; GD 174; Law; mechanics lien
defendant; 1871 Jan; pg 185; GD 176; Law; attachment
defendant; 1871 Jan; pg 185; GD 175; Law; mechanics lien
defendant; 1871 Jan; pg 186; GD 177; Law; mechanics lien
defendant; 1871 Jan; pg 186; GD 178; Law; attachment
defendant; 1871 Jan; pg 187; GD 184; Law; mechanics lien
defendant; 1871 Jan; pg 188; GD 200; Law; trespass on the case of premesis, attachment
defendant; 1871 Jan; pg 188; GD 201; Law; attachment
plaintiff; 1871 Jan; pg 189; GD 202; Law; attachment
defendant; 1871 Jan; pg 189; GD 203; Law; trespass on the case of premesis, damages $8000, attachment
defendant; 1871 June; pg 222; GD 175; Law; mechanics lien
defendant; 1871 June; pg 222; GD 177; Law; mechanics lien
defendant; 1871 June; pg 223; GD 169; Law; mechanics lien
defendant; 1871 June; pg 223; GD 184; Law; mechanics lien
defendant; 1871 June; pg 224; GD 174; Law; mechanics lien
defendant; 1871 June; pg 224; GD 171; Law; mechanics lien

Affolter, Frederick
defendant; 1867 Mar; pg 10; Law; appeal

Akins, Lafayette
defendant; 1868 Mar; pg 78; GD 85; Criminal; indictment for larceny

Akins, Samuel
defendant; 1867 Mar; pg 19; Law; attachment

Alford, William B
defendant; 1871 Jan; pg 193; GD 216; Law; plea of debt, damages $700

Allen, A N
plaintiff; 1872 Jan; pg 254; GD 280; Law; appeal

Allen, A P
defendant; 1869 Jan; pg 105; GD 78; [Law]; trespass, $5000 damages

Allen, Alex P
defendant; [1868 July]; pg 93; GD 97; Law; trespass
defendant; [1868 July]; pg 93; GD 96; Law; trespass
defendant; 1868 July; pg 94; GD 99; Law; trespass
defendant; 1868 July; pg 95; GD 100; Law; trespass
defendant; 1868 July; pg 95; GD 101; Law; trespass
defendant; 1868 July; pg 96; GD 103; Law; [trespass]
defendant; 1868 July; pg 96; GD 102; Law; trespass
defendant; 1868 July; pg 97; GD 104; Law; trespass
defendant; 1868 Mar; pg 87; GD 78; Law; trespass
defendant; 1869 July; pg 117; GD 78; Law; trespass, $5000 damages

Allen, Alexander P
defendant; 1868 July; pg 92; GD 95; Law; trespass
defendant; 1868 July; pg 94; GD 98; Law; trespass
defendant; 1868 Mar; pg 87; GD 79; Law; trespass
defendant; 1869 Jan; pg 108; GD 98; [Law]; trespass, $5000 damages
defendant; 1869 July; pg 118; GD 99; Law; trespass, $5000 damages

Allen, Almenia A
defendant; 1869 July; pg 130; GD 149; Law; replevin

Allen, Alonzo
defendant; 1869 July; pg 123; GD 129; Law; assumpsit

Allen, Oscar
defendant; 1872 Jan; pg 262; GD 301; Law; replevin

Allman, Charles
defendant; 1871 Jan; pg 195; GD 221; Law; appeal

Allum, Jesse F
plaintiff; 1870 Jan; pg 156; GD 175; Law; mechanics lien
plaintiff; 1870 Jan; pg 157; GD 176; Law; attachment
plaintiff; 1871 Jan; pg 185; GD 175; Law; mechanics lien
plaintiff; 1871 Jan; pg 185; GD 176; Law; attachment
plaintiff; 1871 June; pg 222; GD 175; Law; mechanics lien

Altmark, Jacob
defendant; 1871 Jan; pg 195; GD 220; Law; appeal

Amthor, Barnabas B
plaintiff; 1871 Jan; pg 193; GD 216; Law; plea of debt, damages $700

Anderson, Erick
defendant; [1868 July]; pg 93; GD 97; Law; trespass
defendant; [1868 July]; pg 93; GD 96; Law; trespass
defendant; 1868 July; pg 95; GD 100; Law; trespass

Anderson, Erick J
defendant; 1868 July; pg 86; GD 76; Law; appellant
defendant; 1868 July; pg 89; GD 89; Law; replevin
defendant; 1868 July; pg 92; GD 95; Law; trespass
defendant; 1868 July; pg 94; GD 98; Law; trespass
defendant; 1868 July; pg 94; GD 99; Law; trespass
defendant; 1868 July; pg 95; GD 101; Law; trespass
defendant; 1868 July; pg 96; GD 103; Law; [trespass]
defendant; 1868 July; pg 96; GD 102; Law; trespass
defendant; 1868 July; pg 97; GD 104; Law; trespass
defendant; 1868 Mar; pg 72; GD 76; Law; appellant
defendant; 1868 Mar; pg 87; GD 78; Law; trespass
defendant; 1868 Mar; pg 87; GD 79; Law; trespass

defendant; 1868 Mar; pg 88; GD 80; Law; trespass
defendant; 1869 Jan; pg 108; GD 98; [Law]; trespass, $5000 damages
defendant; 1869 July; pg 117; GD 78; Law; trespass, $5000 damages
defendant; 1869 July; pg 118; GD 99; Law; trespass, $5000 damages
defendant; 1869 July; pg 127; GD 143; Law; replevin
defendant; 1869 July; pg 129; GD 146; Law; replevin

Anderson, Jonas
plaintiff; 1871 Jan; pg 190; GD 205; Law; appeal

Anderson, Jonas Jr
defendant; [1868 July]; pg 93; GD 96; Law; trespass
defendant; [1868 July]; pg 93; GD 97; Law; trespass
defendant; 1868 July; pg 92; GD 95; Law; trespass
defendant; 1868 July; pg 94; GD 98; Law; trespass
defendant; 1868 July; pg 94; GD 99; Law; trespass
defendant; 1868 July; pg 95; GD 101; Law; trespass
defendant; 1868 July; pg 95; GD 100; Law; trespass
defendant; 1868 July; pg 96; GD 102; Law; trespass
defendant; 1868 July; pg 96; GD 103; Law; [trespass]
defendant; 1868 July; pg 97; GD 104; Law; trespass

Anderson, Jonas Jr, cont.
defendant; 1869 Jan; pg 108; GD 98; [Law]; trespass, $5000 damages
defendant; 1869 July; pg 118; GD 99; Law; trespass, $5000 damages

Anderson, Jonas Sr
defendant; [1868 July]; pg 93; GD 97; Law; trespass
defendant; [1868 July]; pg 93; GD 96; Law; trespass
defendant; 1868 July; pg 92; GD 95; Law; trespass
defendant; 1868 July; pg 94; GD 98; Law; trespass
defendant; 1868 July; pg 94; GD 99; Law; trespass
defendant; 1868 July; pg 95; GD 101; Law; trespass
defendant; 1868 July; pg 95; GD 100; Law; trespass
defendant; 1868 July; pg 96; GD 103; Law; [trespass]
defendant; 1868 July; pg 96; GD 102; Law; trespass
defendant; 1868 July; pg 97; GD 104; Law; trespass
defendant; 1869 Jan; pg 108; GD 98; [Law]; trespass, $5000 damages
defendant; 1869 July; pg 118; GD 99; Law; trespass, $5000 damages

Andrews, E H
defendant; 1867 Nov; pg 46; GD 38; Law; appeal
defendant; 1868 Mar; pg 79; GD 87; Civil; appeal

Andrews, Elijah H
defendant; 1867 Mar; pg 29; Law; appeal
defendant; 1868 Mar; pg 64; GD 38; Law; appellant
defendant; 1871 Jan; pg 196; GD 222; Law; appeal

Arnett
defendant; 1869 Jan; pg 109; GD 118; [Law]; debt $1000, damages $5000

Arnett, Anthony
plaintiff; 1867 Nov; pg 51; GD 53; Law; attachment
defendant; 1868 July; pg 86; GD 75; Law; appellant
plaintiff; 1868 Mar; pg 66; GD 53; Law; attachment
defendant; 1868 Mar; pg 72; GD 75; Law; appellant
plaintiff; 1869 Jan; pg 113; GD 122; Chancery; for specific performance
plaintiff; 1869 July; pg 122; GD 127; Law; appeal
defendant; 1869 July; pg 130; GD 148; Law; debt $1000, damages $5000
plaintiff; 1870 Jan; pg 144; GD 127; Law; appeal
defendant; 1870 Jan; pg 147; GD 148; Law; debt $1000, damages $5000
plaintiff; 1870 Jan; pg 148; GD 159; Law; attachment
defendant; 1870 Jan; pg 160; GD 183; Law; assumpsit
plaintiff; 1871 Jan; pg 189; GD 203; Law; trespass on the case

of premesis, damages $8000, attachment

plaintiff; 1871 Jan; pg 191; GD 213; Law; trespass damages $1000

plaintiff; 1872 Jan; pg 259; GD 297; Law; assumpsit, damage $1000

B

Bacon, Frank
defendant; 1868 July; pg 84; GD 69; Law; mechanic lien
defendant; 1868 Mar; pg 69; GD 69; Law; mechanic lien
defendant; 1869 July; pg 120; GD 69; Law; mechanics lien

Bailey, Elias
plaintiff; 1867 Mar; pg 36; Chancery; injunction and trespass

Bailey, John C
defendant; 1870 Jan; pg 161; GD 185; Law; assumpsit, damages $1000

Bailey, Stephen
plaintiff; 1872 Jan; pg 255; GD 281; Law; trespass on the case of premises, damages $2000

Baker, Geo W
plaintiff; 1869 Jan; pg 109; GD 119; [Law]; assumpsit

Baldwin, William W
plaintiff; 1871 June; pg 236; GD 265; Chancery; bill for foreclosure
plaintiff; 1872 Jan; pg 264; GD 265; Chancery; bill for foreclosure of mortgage

Barber, Charles E
defendant; 1871 June; pg 216; GD 278; Criminal; indictment for assault with intent to murder
defendant; 1872 Jan; pg 243; GD 278; Criminal; indictment for assault with intent to murder

Barber, Jonas
plaintiff; 1872 Jan; pg 249; GD 269; Law; appeal

Bard
attorney for plaintiff; 1872 Jan; pg 265; GD 268; Chancery; writ of injunction

Bard, Calvin
defendant; 1871 Jan; pg 176; Criminal
defendant; 1871 Jan; pg 177; GD 237; Criminal; assault &c
defendant; 1871 June; pg 214; GD 238; Criminal; indictment for larceny
defendant; 1871 June; pg 214; GD 237; Criminal; indictment for assault with intent to kill

Bard, E M
defendant; 1871 Jan; pg 203; GD 224; Chancery
Baries, S M
attorney for plaintiff; 1871 June; pg 236; GD 268; Chancery; a writ of injunction

Barker, Amander
defendant; 1867 Mar; pg 30; Law; assumpsit
defendant; 1867 Nov; pg 46; GD 35; Law; assumpsit

Barker, Amander, cont.
defendant; 1871 Jan; pg 192; GD
215; Law; assumpsit, damages
$300

Barter, John
defendant; 1867 Mar; pg 18; Law;
trespass

Bates, Joseph E
plaintiff; 1869 July; pg 126; GD
139; Law; assumpsit, damages
$1000

Beach, E N
defendant; 1871 June; pg 226; GD
261; Law; attachment
defendant; 1872 Jan; pg 248; GD
261; Law; attachment

Beales, John W
defendant; 1871 June; pg 223; GD
184; Law; mechanics lien

Beckwith (Smith & Beckwith)
defendant; 1871 June; pg 225; GD
258; Law; assumpsit, damages
$2000

Beckwith, Fred C
plaintiff; 1871 June; pg 232; GD
212; Chancery; bill for exceeding their authority and other
illegal proceedings

Beckwith, Frederick C
defendant; 1868 July; pg 92; GD
94; Law; trespass
defendant; 1869 Jan; pg 107; GD
94; [Law]; assumpsit
plaintiff; 1871 Jan; pg 202; GD
212; Chancery; bill for exceeding their authority and other
illegal proceedings

plaintiff; 1872 Jan; pg 263; GD
212; Chancery; bill for exceeding their authority and other
illegal proceedings

Beckwith, George C
defendant; 1867 Mar; pg 11; Law;
appeal

Beckwith, George L
defendant; 1871 June; pg 225; GD
259; Law; assumpsit, damages
$2000
defendant; 1871 June; pg 225; GD
258; Law; assumpsit, damages
$2000

Beckwith, Lawson
defendant; 1868 July; pg 92; GD
94; Law; trespass
defendant; 1869 Jan; pg 107; GD
94; [Law]; assumpsit
defendant; 1869 Jan; pg 110; GD
113; [Law]; appeal
defendant; 1871 June; pg 225; GD
259; Law; assumpsit, damages
$2000

Beckwith, Louise P
defendant; 1872 Jan; pg 254; GD
280; Law; appeal

Beckwith, Oscar F
defendant; 1871 June; pg 225; GD
258; Law; assumpsit, damages
$2000

Bell, Henry
plaintiff; 1867 Nov; pg 54; GD 61;
Law; appeal

Benedict
attorney for plaintiff; 1870 Jan; pg
163; GD 135; Chancery; foreclosure

Berger, Samuel
  defendant; 1867 Nov; pg 38; GD
    41; Criminal; assault with intent
    to inflict bodily injury
  defendant; 1868 Mar; pg 60; GD
    41; Criminal; assault with intent
    to inflict bodily injury

Berk[ley], G
  attorney for plaintiff; 1870 Jan; pg
    155; GD 173; Law; attachment

Berkley
  attorney for defendant; 1867 Nov;
    pg 42; GD 6; Law; appeal at issue
  attorney for defendant; 1867 Nov;
    pg 42; GD 14; Law; replevin
    appeal
  attorney for plaintiff; 1867 Nov; pg
    44; GD 31
  attorney for defendant; 1867 Nov;
    pg 44; GD 30; trespass at issue
  attorney for plaintiff; 1867 Nov; pg
    45; GD 36; Law; assumpsit
  attorney for plaintiff; 1867 Nov; pg
    45; GD 32; Law; appeal
  attorney for plaintiff; 1867 Nov; pg
    46; GD 38; Law; appeal
  attorney for defendant; 1867 Nov;
    pg 48; GD 47; Law
  attorney for defendant; 1867 Nov;
    pg 48; GD 48; Law; trespass
  attorney for defendant; 1867 Nov;
    pg 49; GD 51; Law
  attorney for defendant; 1867 Nov;
    pg 50; GD 53; Law; Appeal
  attorney for defendant; 1867 Nov;
    pg 50; GD 52; Law; replevin
  attorney for defendant; 1867 Nov;
    pg 51; GD 54; Law; mechanic
    lien

attorney for plaintiff; 1867 Nov; pg
    51; GD 53; Law; attachment
attorney for plaintiff; 1867 Nov; pg
    52; GD 55; Law; mechanic lien
attorney for defendant; 1867 Nov;
    pg 53; GD 58; Law; assumpsit
attorney for plaintiff; 1867 Nov; pg
    54; Law; appeal
attorney for defendant; 1867 Nov;
    pg 54; GD 9; Law; replevin, at
    issue
attorney for defendant; 1867 Nov;
    pg 55; GD 13; Chancery; fore-
    closure of mortgage
attorney for defendant; 1867 Nov;
    pg 56; GD 64; Chancery; injunc-
    tion
attorney for defendant; 1868 July;
    pg 85; GD 70; Law; assumpsit
attorney for plaintiff; 1868 July; pg
    89; GD 89; Law; replevin
attorney for defendant; 1868 July;
    pg 90; GD 91; Law; attachment
attorney for plaintiff; 1868 July; pg
    90; GD 90; Law; covenant
attorney for plaintiff; 1868 July; pg
    91; GD 92; Law; trespass
attorney for defendant; 1868 Mar;
    pg 62; GD 14; Law; replevin
attorney for plaintiff; 1868 Mar; pg
    64; GD 38; Law; appellant
attorney for defendant; 1868 Mar;
    pg 65; GD 48; Law; trespass
attorney for defendant; 1868 Mar;
    pg 66; GD 52; Law; appellant
attorney for plaintiff; 1868 Mar; pg
    66; GD 53; Law; attachment
attorney for plaintiff; 1868 Mar; pg
    67; GD 55; Law; mechanic lien

Berkley, cont.

attorney for defendant; 1868 Mar; pg 69; GD 70; Law; assumpsit

attorney for plaintiff; 1868 Mar; pg 70; GD 72; Law; debt

attorney for defendant; 1868 Mar; pg 73; GD 78; Law; trespass

attorney for defendant; 1868 Mar; pg 73; GD 77; Law; appellant

attorney for defendant; 1868 Mar; pg 75; GD 81; Law; trespass

attorney for defendant; 1868 Mar; pg 75; GD 82; Law; effectment

attorney for plaintiff; 1868 Mar; pg 76; GD 83; Law; appellant

attorney for defendant; 1868 Mar; pg 77; GD 62; Chancery; foreclosure of mortgage

attorney for plaintiff; 1868 Mar; pg 79; GD 87; Civil; appeal

attorney for defendant; 1869 Jan; pg 102; GD 67; Criminal; indictment for obstructing high way

attorney for defendant; 1869 Jan; pg 104; GD 117; Criminal; assault & battery, appealed from Justice

attorney for defendant; 1869 Jan; pg 105; GD 78; [Law]; trespass, $5000 damages

attorney for defendant; 1869 Jan; pg 106; GD 91; [Law]; attachment

attorney for defendant; 1869 Jan; pg 107; GD 94; [Law]; assumpsit

attorney for plaintiff; 1869 Jan; pg 107; GD 92; [Law]; assumpsit

attorney for plaintiff; 1869 Jan; pg 108; GD 112; [Law]; attachment

attorney for plaintiff; 1869 Jan; pg 109; GD 119; [Law]; assumpsit

attorney for defendant; 1869 Jan; pg 110; GD 120; [Law]; appeal

attorney for plaintiff; 1869 July; pg 119; GD 112; Law; attachment

attorney for plaintiff; 1869 July; pg 121; GD 124; Law; appeal

attorney for plaintiff; 1869 July; pg 121; GD 125; Law; mechanics lien

attorney for plaintiff; 1869 July; pg 122; GD 127; Law; appeal

attorney for plaintiff; 1869 July; pg 122; GD 126; Law; mechanics lien

attorney for plaintiff; 1869 July; pg 123; GD 128; Law; mechanics lien

attorney for plaintiff; 1869 July; pg 124; GD 136; Law; attachment

attorney for plaintiff; 1869 July; pg 124; GD 132; Law; attachment

attorney for plaintiff; 1869 July; pg 125; GD 138; Law; mechanics lien

attorney for plaintiff; 1869 July; pg 125; GD 137; Law; action debt $1000, damages $1000

attorney for plaintiff; 1869 July; pg 126; GD 139; Law; assumpsit, damages $1000

attorney for plaintiff; 1869 July; pg 126; GD 141; Law; assumpsit, damage $2000

attorney for plaintiff; 1869 July; pg 127; GD 143; Law; replevin

attorney for plaintiff; 1869 July; pg 128; GD 144; Law; mechanics lien attorney for defendant; 1869 July; pg 128; GD 145; Law; appeal

attorney for defendant; 1869 July; pg 130; GD 149; Law; replevin

attorney for plaintiff; 1869 July; pg 130; GD 148; Law; debt $1000, damages $5000

attorney for plaintiff; 1869 July; pg 131; GD 150; Law; mechanics lien

attorney for plaintiff; 1869 July; pg 131; GD 151; Law; appeal

attorney for plaintiff; 1869 July; pg 132; GD 152; Law; mechanics lien

attorney for plaintiff; 1869 July; pg 134; GD 121; Chancery; divorce

attorney for plaintiff; 1869 July; pg 135; GD 133; Chancery; foreclo-sure of mortgage

attorney for defendant; 1869 July; pg 136; GD 134; Chancery

attorney for plaintiff; 1869 July; pg 137; GD 140; Chancery; divorce

attorney for defendant; 1870 Jan; pg 146; GD 145; Law; appeal

attorney for plaintiff; 1870 Jan; pg 148; GD 152; Law; mechanics lien

attorney for plaintiff; 1870 Jan; pg 153; GD 168; Law; appeal

attorney for defendant; 1870 Jan; pg 158; GD 179; Law; replevin

attorney for defendant; 1870 Jan; pg 159; GD 180; Law; appeal

attorney for plaintiff; 1870 Jan; pg 159; GD 181; Law; trespass on the case upon premises, dam-ages $1000

attorney for defendant; 1870 Jan; pg 160; GD 182; Law; assumpsit

attorney for plaintiff; 1870 Jan; pg 162; GD 158; Chancery

attorney for plaintiff; 1870 Jan; pg 162; GD 133; Chancery; foreclo-sure

attorney for plaintiff; 1870 Jan; pg 163; GD 140; Chancery; divorce

attorney for defendant; 1871 June; pg 217; GD 250; Law; debt $3000, damages $3000

attorney for defendant; 1872 Jan; pg 255; GD 281; Law; trespass on the case of premises, dam-ages $2000

Berkley & Brown

attorney for plaintiff; 1871 June; pg 219; GD 126; Law; mechan-ics lien

attorney for plaintiff; 1871 June; pg 220; GD 152; Law; mechan-ics lien

attorney for plaintiff; 1871 June; pg 223; GD 169; Law; mechan-ics lien

attorney for plaintiff; 1871 June; pg 224; GD 171; Law; mechan-ics lien

attorney for plaintiff; 1871 June; pg 224; GD 174; Law; mechan-ics lien

attorney for plaintiff; 1871 June; pg 232; GD 212; Chancery; bill for exceeding their authority and other illegal proceedings

Berkley & Decker

attorney for plaintiff; 1871 June; pg 233; GD 158; Chancery; divorce

Berkley & Wright

attorney for defendant; 1868 Mar; pg 68; GD 58; Law; assumpsit

attorney for plaintiff; 1868 Mar; pg 70; GD 71; Law; trespass

attorney for defendant; 1869 July; pg 116; GD 110; Criminal; murder

Berkley (Brown & Berkley)

attorney for plaintiff; 1871 June; pg 218; GD 128; Law; mechanics lien

attorney for plaintiff; 1871 June; pg 218; GD 126; Law; mechanics lien

Berkley (Decker & Berkley)

attorney for plaintiff; 1872 Jan; pg 267; GD 255; Chancery; divorce

Berkley (Wright & Berkley)

attorney for plaintiff; 1868 July; pg 85; GD 71; Law; trespass

attorney for defendant; 1868 July; pg 86; GD 76; Law; appellant

attorney for defendant; 1868 July; pg 86; GD 75; Law; appellant

attorney for defendant; 1869 Jan; pg 108; GD 98; [Law]; trespass, $5000 damages

attorney for plaintiff; 1871 Jan; pg 193; GD 217; Law; appeal

Berkley, Brown & Putman

attorney for plaintiff; 1872 Jan; pg 246; GD 150; Law; mechanics lien

attorney for plaintiff; 1872 Jan; pg 246; GD 125; Law; mechanics lien

attorney for defendant; 1872 Jan; pg 247; GD 128; Law; mechanics lien

attorney for defendant; 1872 Jan; pg 251; GD 263; Law; trespass, damages $2000

attorney for defendant; 1872 Jan; pg 251; GD 266; Law; unlawful forcible entry & detainer

attorney for plaintiff; 1872 Jan; pg 263; GD 212; Chancery; bill for exceeding their authority and other illegal proceedings

attorney for defendant; 1872 Jan; pg 265; GD 291; Chancery; writ of injunction

Berkley, G

attorney for defendant; [1872 Jan]; pg 319; GD 145; Law; appeal

attorney for plaintiff; 1868 July; pg 82; GD 36; Law; assumpsit

attorney for defendant; 1868 July; pg 82; GD 52; Law; appellant

attorney for plaintiff; 1868 July; pg 83; GD 54; Law; mechanic lien

attorney for plaintiff; 1868 July; pg 83; GD 55; Law; mechanic lien

attorney for defendant; 1868 Mar; pg 63; GD 30; Law; trespass

attorney for plaintiff; 1868 Mar; pg 63; GD 36; Law; assumpsit

attorney for defendant; 1869 Jan; pg 112; GD 111; Chancery; divorce

attorney for plaintiff; 1869 Jan; pg 113; GD 121; Chancery; divorce

attorney for plaintiff; 1869 Jan; pg 113; GD 122; Chancery; for specific performance

District Attorney; 1870 Jan; pg 140; Criminal; keeping gaming house

District Attorney; 1870 Jan; pg 140; Criminal; selling liquor without license

attorney for defendant; 1870 Jan; pg 141; GD 110; Criminal; indictment for murder

attorney for defendant; 1870 Jan; pg 142; Criminal; keepig open tippling house on Sabbath

attorney for plaintiff; 1870 Jan; pg 143; GD 126; Law; mechanics lien

attorney for plaintiff; 1870 Jan; pg 143; GD 125; Law; mechanics lien

attorney for plaintiff; 1870 Jan; pg 144; GD 127; Law; appeal

attorney for plaintiff; 1870 Jan; pg 144; GD 128; Law; mechanics lien

attorney for plaintiff; 1870 Jan; pg 145; GD 137; Law; action debt $1000, damages $1000

attorney for plaintiff; 1870 Jan; pg 145; GD 138; Law; mechanics lien

attorney for plaintiff; 1870 Jan; pg 146; GD 141; Law; assumpsit, damages $2000

attorney for plaintiff; 1870 Jan; pg 147; GD 148; Law; debt $1000, damages $5000

attorney for plaintiff; 1870 Jan; pg 147; GD 150; Law; mechanics lien

attorney for plaintiff; 1870 Jan; pg 151; GD 164; Law; attachment

attorney for plaintiff; 1870 Jan; pg 151; GD 165; Law; attachment

attorney for plaintiff; 1870 Jan; pg 152; GD 166; Law; appeal

attorney for plaintiff; 1870 Jan; pg 154; GD 171; Law; mechanics lien

attorney for plaintiff; 1870 Jan; pg 154; [GD 170]; Law; attachment

attorney for plaintiff; 1870 Jan; pg 155; GD 172; Law; attachment

attorney for plaintiff; 1870 Jan; pg 156; GD 174; Law; mechanics lien

attorney for plaintiff; 1870 Jan; pg 156; GD 175; Law; mechanics lien

attorney for plaintiff; 1870 Jan; pg 157; GD 177; Law; mechanics lien

attorney for plaintiff; 1870 Jan; pg 157; GD 176; Law; attachment

attorney for plaintiff; 1870 Jan; pg 158; GD 178; Law; attachment

attorney for plaintiff; 1870 Jan; pg 160; GD 183; Law; assumpsit

attorney for defendant; 1870 Jan; pg 164; GD 134; Chancery; chancery

attorney for defendant; 1870 Jan; pg 168; Criminal; selling liquor without license

attorney for defendant; 1870 Jan; pg 168; Criminal; keeping open tippling house on Sabbath

attorney for defendant; 1870 Jan; pg 169; Criminal; keeping open tippling house on Sabbath

Berkley, G, cont.

attorney for defendant; 1871 Jan; pg 171; GD 110; Criminal; indictment for murder

attorney for plaintiff; 1871 Jan; pg 178; GD 126; Law; mechanics lien

attorney for plaintiff; 1871 Jan; pg 178; GD 125; Law; mechanics lien

attorney for plaintiff; 1871 Jan; pg 179; GD 128; Law; mechanics lien

attorney for plaintiff; 1871 Jan; pg 179; GD 137; Law; motion of debt $1000, damages $1000

attorney for defendant; 1871 Jan; pg 180; GD 145; Law

attorney for plaintiff; 1871 Jan; pg 180; GD 138; Law; mechanics lien

attorney for plaintiff; 1871 Jan; pg 181; GD 152; Law; mechanics lien

attorney for plaintiff; 1871 Jan; pg 181; GD 150; Law; mechanics lien

attorney for plaintiff; 1871 Jan; pg 182; GD 170; Law; attachment

attorney for plaintiff; 1871 Jan; pg 182; GD 169; Law; mechanics lien

attorney for plaintiff; 1871 Jan; pg 183; GD 171; Law; mechanics lien

attorney for plaintiff; 1871 Jan; pg 183; GD 172; Law; attachment

attorney for plaintiff; 1871 Jan; pg 184; GD 174; Law; mechanics lien

attorney for defendant; 1871 Jan; pg 184; GD 173; Law; attachment

attorney for plaintiff; 1871 Jan; pg 185; GD 175; Law; mechanics lien

attorney for plaintiff; 1871 Jan; pg 185; GD 176; Law; attachment

attorney for plaintiff; 1871 Jan; pg 186; GD 177; Law; mechanics lien

attorney for plaintiff; 1871 Jan; pg 186; GD 178; Law; attachment

attorney for plaintiff; 1871 Jan; pg 187; GD 181; Law; trespass on the case upon premises, damages $1000

attorney for plaintiff; 1871 Jan; pg 190; GD 205; Law; appeal

attorney for defendant; 1871 Jan; pg 190; GD 206; Law; appeal

attorney for plaintiff; 1871 Jan; pg 191; GD 207; Law; trespass damages $2000

attorney for plaintiff; 1871 Jan; pg 191; GD 213; Law; trespass damages $1000

attorney for defendant; 1871 Jan; pg 195; GD 221; Law; appeal

attorney for plaintiff; 1871 Jan; pg 196; GD 225; Law; appeal

attorney for defendant; 1871 Jan; pg 197; GD 227; Law; debt, $600

attorney for plaintiff; 1871 Jan; pg 198; GD 230; Law

attorney for plaintiff; 1871 Jan; pg 199; GD 158; Chancery

attorney for plaintiff; 1871 Jan; pg 199; GD 133; Chancery; foreclosure of mortgage attorney for plaintiff; 1871 Jan; pg 200; GD 204; Chancery; foreclosure of mortgage

attorney for plaintiff; 1871 Jan; pg 200; GD 210; Chancery; foreclosure of mortgage

attorney for plaintiff; 1871 Jan; pg 201; GD 211; Chancery; foreclosure of mortgage

attorney for plaintiff; 1871 Jan; pg 202; GD 212; Chancery; bill for exceeding their authority and other illegal proceedings

attorney for plaintiff; 1871 Jan; pg 203; GD 223; Chancery; divorce

attorney for plaintiff; 1871 June; pg 217; GD 254; Law

attorney for plaintiff; 1871 June; pg 219; GD 150; Law; mechanics lien

attorney for defendant; 1871 June; pg 221; GD 227; Law; debt $600, damages $600

attorney for plaintiff; 1871 June; pg 222; GD 177; Law; mechanics lien

attorney for plaintiff; 1871 June; pg 222; GD 175; Law; mechanics lien

attorney for plaintiff; 1871 June; pg 226; GD 262; Law; trespass

attorney for plaintiff; 1871 June; pg 227; GD 137; Law; actions of debt, damages $1000

attorney for plaintiff; 1871 June; pg 228; GD 267; Law; trespass on premesis, damages $3000, suit withdrawn by plaintiff

attorney for plaintiff; 1871 June; pg 229; GD 269; Law; appeal

attorney for plaintiff; 1871 June; pg 232; GD 223; Chancery; bill for divorce and for confirmation of masters sale

attorney for plaintiff; 1871 June; pg 233; GD 158; Chancery; injunction

attorney for plaintiff; 1871 June; pg 234; GD 256; Chancery; divorce

attorney for plaintiff; 1871 June; pg 235; GD 260; Chancery; divorce

attorney for plaintiff; 1871 June; pg 235; GD 264; Chancery; a writ of injunction

attorney for defendant; 1872 Jan; pg 240; GD 244; Criminal; indictment for setting timber on fire

attorney for plaintiff; 1872 Jan; pg 249; GD 269; Law; appeal

attorney for defendant; 1872 Jan; pg 252; GD 272; Law; assumpsit, damages $500

attorney for plaintiff; 1872 Jan; pg 252; GD 262; Law; trespass

attorney for plaintiff; 1872 Jan; pg 253; GD 137; Law; action of debt, damages $100

attorney for defendant; 1872 Jan; pg 254; GD 227; Law; debt, $600, damage $600

attorney for defendant; 1872 Jan; pg 254; GD 280; Law; appeal

attorney for plaintiff; 1872 Jan; pg 255; GD 282; Law; appeal

attorney for plaintiff; 1872 Jan; pg 256; GD 289; Law; assumpsit, damages $400

Berkley, G, cont.

attorney for plaintiff; 1872 Jan; pg 256; GD 288; Law; assumpsit, damages $1500

attorney for plaintiff; 1872 Jan; pg 257; GD 290; Law; assumpsit, damages $200

attorney for defendant; 1872 Jan; pg 258; GD 294; Law; appeal

attorney for plaintiff; 1872 Jan; pg 261; GD 301; Law; mechanics lien

attorney for defendant; 1872 Jan; pg 262; GD 301; Law; appeal

attorney for plaintiff; 1872 Jan; pg 262; GD 302; Law; mechanics lien

attorney for plaintiff; 1872 Jan; pg 263; GD 158; Chancery; injunction

attorney for plaintiff; 1872 Jan; pg 264; GD 264; Chancery; writ of injunction

attorney for plaintiff; 1872 Jan; pg 269; GD 295; Chancery; divorce

Berkley, Granville

defendant; [1872 Jan]; pg 319; GD 145; Law; appeal

plaintiff; 1868 Mar; pg 79; GD 87; Civil; appeal

defendant; 1869 July; pg 128; GD 145; Law; appeal

defendant; 1870 Jan; pg 146; GD 145; Law; appeal

plaintiff; 1870 Jan; pg 159; GD 181; Law; trespass on the case upon premises, damages $1000

plaintiff; 1871 Jan; pg 180; GD 145; Law

plaintiff; 1871 Jan; pg 187; GD 181; Law; trespass on the case upon premises, damages $1000

defendant; 1871 Jan; pg 193; GD 216; Law; plea of debt, damages $700

plaintiff; 1871 Jan; pg 198; GD 230; Law

plaintiff; 1871 Jan; pg 202; GD 212; Chancery; bill for exceeding their authority and other illegal proceedings

plaintiff; 1871 June; pg 232; GD 212; Chancery; bill for exceeding their authority and other illegal proceedings

plaintiff; 1872 Jan; pg 263; GD 212; Chancery; bill for exceeding their authority and other illegal proceedings

Berkley, Junius

defendant; 1867 Nov; pg 57; Criminal; indictment for murder

Berkley, S

attorney for plaintiff; 1870 Jan; pg 153; GD 169; Law; mechanics lien

Besler, John W

defendant; 1871 Jan; pg 187; GD 184; Law; mechanics lien

Bestle, Gottlieb

plaintiff; 1868 July; pg 89; GD 88; Law; trespass

Bishop, Charles

defendant; 1867 Nov; pg 40; GD 45; Criminal; indictment for larceny

Brett, Mathew D

plaintiff; 1872 Jan; pg 261; GD 301; Law; mechanics lien

Bristol, James

defendant; 1868 July; pg 100; GD 108; Law [Criminal]; indictment for larceny

defendant; 1869 Jan; pg 103; GD 108; Criminal; indictment for larceny

defendant; 1869 July; pg 116; GD 108; Criminal; larceny

defendant; 1870 Jan; pg 139; GD 108; Criminal; indictment for malicious mischief

Brown

attorney for plaintiff; 1867 Nov; pg 43; GD 27; Law; replevin

attorney for defendant; 1867 Nov; pg 45; GD 32; Law; appeal

attorney for plaintiff; 1869 July; pg 129; GD 147; Law; assumpsit, Damages $500

attorney for plaintiff; 1871 Jan; pg 202; GD 212; Chancery; bill for exceeding their authority and other illegal proceedings

attorney for plaintiff; 1871 June; pg 219; GD 150; Law; mechanics lien

attorney for plaintiff; 1871 June; pg 222; GD 175; Law; mechanics lien

attorney for plaintiff; 1871 June; pg 222; GD 177; Law; mechanics lien

Brown & Berkley

attorney for plaintiff; 1871 June; pg 218; GD 126; Law; mechanics lien

attorney for plaintiff; 1871 June; pg 218; GD 128; Law; mechanics lien

Brown & Hunt

attorney for plaintiff; 1867 Nov; pg 54; GD 9; Law; replevin, at issue

Brown & Putman

attorney for plaintiff; 1871 June; pg 226; GD 261; Law; attachment

attorney for plaintiff; 1872 Jan; pg 248; GD 261; Law; attachment

attorney for defendant; 1872 Jan; pg 249; GD 269; Law; appeal

attorney for plaintiff; 1872 Jan; pg 250; GD 250; Law; debt $3000, damages $3000

Brown (Berkley & Brown)

attorney for plaintiff; 1871 June; pg 219; GD 126; Law; mechanics lien

attorney for plaintiff; 1871 June; pg 220; GD 152; Law; mechanics lien

attorney for plaintiff; 1871 June; pg 223; GD 169; Law; mechanics lien

attorney for plaintiff; 1871 June; pg 224; GD 174; Law; mechanics lien

attorney for plaintiff; 1871 June; pg 224; GD 171; Law; mechanics lien

attorney for plaintiff; 1871 June; pg 232; GD 212; Chancery; bill for

Brown, Nathan W
  defendant; 1871 June; pg 216; GD 279; Criminal; indictment for selling liquor without a license
  defendant; 1871 June; pg 226; GD 262; Law; trespass
  defendant; 1871 June; pg 235; GD 264; Chancery; a writ of injunction
  defendant; 1872 Jan; pg 244; GD 279; Criminal; indictment for selling liquor without a license
  defendant; 1872 Jan; pg 252; GD 262; Law; trespass
  defendant; 1872 Jan; pg 260; GD 298; Law; assumpsit, damages $300
  defendant; 1872 Jan; pg 264; GD 264; Chancery; writ of injunction

Brown, S E
  attorney for plaintiff; 1871 June; pg 217; GD 250; Law; debt $3000, damages $3000
  attorney for defendant; 1871 June; pg 229; GD 269; Law; appeal
  attorney for defendant; 1871 June; pg 233; GD 158; Chancery; injunction

Brown, Samuel E
  plaintiff; 1871 June; pg 226; GD 261; Law; attachment
  plaintiff; 1872 Jan; pg 248; GD 261; Law; attachment

Browne
  attorney for plaintiff; 1867 Nov; pg 42; GD 6; Law; appeal at issue
  attorney for defendant; 1867 Nov; pg 45; GD 36; Law; assumpsit
  attorney for plaintiff; 1867 Nov; pg 48; GD 48; Law; trespass
  attorney for plaintiff; 1867 Nov; pg 50; GD 52; Law; replevin
  attorney for plaintiff; 1867 Nov; pg 53; GD 58; Law; assumpsit
  attorney for plaintiff; 1867 Nov; pg 54; GD 60; Law; mechanic lien
  attorney for plaintiff; 1867 Nov; pg 55; GD 13; Chancery; foreclosure of mortgage
  attorney for defendant; 1867 Nov; pg 56; GD 64; Chancery; injunction
  attorney for plaintiff; 1868 Mar; pg 68; GD 58; Law; assumpsit
  attorney for plaintiff; 1870 Jan; pg 149; GD 160; Law; replevin

Browne & Hunt
  attorney for plaintiff; 1867 Nov; pg 48; GD 47; Law
  Browne (Post, Browne & others)
  attorney for plaintiff; 1868 Mar; pg 88; GD 81; Law; trespass

Browne (Teller & Browne)
  attorney for defendant; 1868 Mar; pg 88; GD 81; Law; trespass

Browne, Decker & Wright
  attorney for defendant; 1870 Jan; pg 162; GD 158; Chancery
  Bruce, Jacob
  defendant; 1867 Mar; pg 7; Law; replevin
  defendant; 1867 Nov; pg 48; GD 47; Law; debt
  defendant; 1867 Nov; pg 54; GD 9; Law; replevin, at issue

Carr, James A, cont.

defendant; 1867 Mar; pg 28; Law; assumpsit

defendant; 1867 Nov; pg 45; GD 36; Law; assumpsit

defendant; 1868 Mar; pg 63; GD 36; Law; assumpsit

Carr, S H

plaintiff; 1867 Mar; pg 17; Law; appeal by certiorari

Carroll, James

plaintiff; 1868 Mar; pg 74; GD 79; Law; trespass

plaintiff; 1868 Mar; pg 87; GD 79; Law; trespass

Carter, Henry L

plaintiff; 1871 Jan; pg 192; GD 215; Law; assumpsit, damages $300

Carter, John C

defendant; 1867 Mar; pg 2; Criminal; indictment

defendant; 1867 Mar; pg 6; Law; appeal

defendant; 1869 July; pg 124; GD 136; Law; attachment

Chace, Geo F

defendant; 1871 June; pg 232; GD 212; Chancery; bill for exceeding their authority and other illegal proceedings

Chamberlain, G W

attorney for defendant; 1870 Jan; pg 144; GD 127; Law; appeal

attorney for defendant; 1870 Jan; pg 145; GD 137; Law; action debt $1000, damages $1000

attorney for defendant; 1870 Jan; pg 152; GD 166; Law; appeal

Chamberlain, George W

plaintiff; 1871 June; pg 225; GD 259; Law; assumpsit, damages $2000

Chamberlain, William S

plaintiff; 1870 Jan; pg 162; GD 158; Chancery

defendant; 1871 June; pg 217; GD 250; Law; debt $3000, damages $3000

plaintiff; 1871 June; pg 233; GD 158; Chancery; injunction

defendant; 1872 Jan; pg 250; GD 250; Law; debt $3000, damages $3000

plaintiff; 1872 Jan; pg 263; GD 158; Chancery; injunction

plaintiff; 1871 Jan; pg 199; GD 158; Chancery

Chambers (Campbell & Chambers)

defendant; 1867 Nov; pg 56; GD 62; Chancery; foreclosure of mortgage

Chambers, Geo W

defendant; 1869 Jan; pg 109; GD 119; [Law]; assumpsit

Chambers, George W

defendant; 1867 Mar; pg 13; Law; appeal

defendant; 1868 Mar; pg 77; GD 62; Chancery; foreclosure of mortgage

defendant; 1872 Jan; pg 256; GD 288; Law; assumpsit, damages $1500

Chapman, E W

defendant; 1871 June; pg 225; GD

259; Law; assumpsit, damages
$2000

Chapman, Eric

defendant; 1867 Mar; pg 9; Law;
appeal

Charles

attorney for plaintiff; 1868 Mar; pg
62; GD 29; Law; trespass
attorney for plaintiff; 1869 July; pg
120; GD 29; Law; assumpsit

Charles & Elbert

attorney for plaintiff; 1872 Jan; pg
255; GD 281; Law; trespass on
the case of premises, damages
$2000

Chase, George F

defendant; 1870 Jan; pg 159; GD
181; Law; trespass on the case
upon premises, damages $1000
defendant; 1871 Jan; pg 187; GD
181; Law; trespass on the case
upon premises, damages $1000
defendant; 1871 Jan; pg 202; GD
212; Chancery; bill for exceeding their authority and other
illegal proceedings
defendant; 1872 Jan; pg 263; GD
212; Chancery; bill for exceeding their authority and other
illegal proceedings

Church, George H

plaintiff; 1869 July; pg 123; GD
130; Law; assumpsit
plaintiff; 1869 July; pg 123; GD
129; Law; assumpsit

Clapp, Rufus

plaintiff; 1871 Jan; pg 205; GD 234;

Law; appeal, change of venue
from Gilpin County

Clark, James

plaintiff; 1872 Jan; pg 260; GD 299;
Law; assumpsit, damage, $1200

Clements, Alfred H

plaintiff; 1868 July; pg 85; GD 71;
Law; trespass
plaintiff; 1868 Mar; pg 70; GD 71;
Law; trespass

Clements, Court C

plaintiff; 1872 Jan; pg 266; GD 285;
Chancery; bill for foreclosure of
mortgage

Clements, Henry

defendant; 1872 Jan; pg 266; GD
285; Chancery; bill for foreclosure of mortgage

Cluff, C P

defendant; 1868 July; pg 85; GD
71; Law; trespass
defendant; 1871 Jan; pg 202; GD
212; Chancery; bill for exceeding their authority and other
illegal proceedings
defendant; 1871 June; pg 232; GD
212; Chancery; bill for exceeding their authority and other
illegal proceedings
defendant; 1872 Jan; pg 263; GD
212; Chancery; bill for exceeding their authority and other
illegal proceedings

Cocoman, Michael

plaintiff; 1872 Jan; pg 258; GD
294; Law; appeal

Cofield, Joseph
plaintiff; 1867 Nov; pg 53; GD 59;
Law; attachment

Cofman [Coffman], E J
defendant; 1867 Mar; pg 17; Law;
appeal by certiorari

Cole, Chester M
plaintiff; 1867 Nov; pg 50; GD 53;
Law; Appeal
plaintiff; 1868 July; pg 82; GD 52;
Law; assumpsit
plaintiff; 1868 Mar; pg 66; GD 52;
Law; appellant

Cole, Leroy
defendant; 1867 Nov; pg 38; GD
41; Criminal; assault with intent
to inflict bodily injury
defendant; 1868 Mar; pg 60; GD
41; Criminal; assault with intent
to inflict bodily injury

Collier, John
plaintiff; 1868 Mar; pg 74; GD 80;
Law; trespass
plaintiff; 1868 Mar; pg 88; GD 80;
Law; trespass

Conoy, Thomas
defendant; 1869 July; pg 136; GD
135; Chancery; foreclosure of
mortgage

Consolidated Gregory Company
defendant; 1871 Jan; pg 197; GD
226; Law; assumpsit
defendant; 1871 Jan; pg 198; GD
231; Law; attachment
defendant; 1871 Jan; pg 198; GD
232; Law; assumpsit

Cook
plaintiff; 1868 Mar; pg 68; GD 60;
Law; mechanic lien

Cook (Perkins & Cook)
attorney for plaintiff; 1867 Nov; pg
56; GD 64; Chancery; injunction
attorney for plaintiff; 1868 Mar; pg
63; GD 30; Law; trespass

Cook, George D
plaintiff; [1872 Jan]; pg 319; GD
60; Law; mechanics lien
plaintiff; 1867 Nov; pg 54; GD 60;
Law; mechanic lien
plaintiff; 1868 July; pg 84; GD 60;
Law; mechanic lien
plaintiff; 1869 Jan; pg 111; GD 60;
[Law]; mechanics lien
plaintiff; 1869 July; pg 119; GD 60;
Law; mechanics lien

Cook, John
plaintiff; 1867 Mar; pg 3; Law;
trespass

Cook, Lyman
defendant; 1870 Jan; pg 153; GD
169; Law; mechanics lien
defendant; 1870 Jan; pg 154; GD
171; Law; mechanics lien
defendant; 1870 Jan; pg 154; [GD
170]; Law; attachment
defendant; 1870 Jan; pg 155; GD
173; Law; attachment
defendant; 1870 Jan; pg 155; GD
172; Law; attachment
defendant; 1870 Jan; pg 156; GD
175; Law; mechanics lien
defendant; 1870 Jan; pg 156; GD
174; Law; mechanics lien

defendant; 1870 Jan; pg 157; GD 176; Law; attachment

defendant; 1870 Jan; pg 157; GD 177; Law; mechanics lien

defendant; 1870 Jan; pg 158; GD 178; Law; attachment

defendant; 1870 Jan; pg 161; GD 184; Law; mechanics lien

defendant; 1871 Jan; pg 182; GD 169; Law; mechanics lien

defendant; 1871 Jan; pg 182; GD 170; Law; attachment

defendant; 1871 Jan; pg 183; GD 171; Law; mechanics lien

defendant; 1871 Jan; pg 183; GD 172; Law; attachment

defendant; 1871 Jan; pg 184; GD 173; Law; attachment

defendant; 1871 Jan; pg 184; GD 174; Law; mechanics lien

defendant; 1871 Jan; pg 185; GD 176; Law; attachment

defendant; 1871 Jan; pg 185; GD 175; Law; mechanics lien

defendant; 1871 Jan; pg 186; GD 178; Law; attachment

defendant; 1871 Jan; pg 186; GD 177; Law; mechanics lien

defendant; 1871 Jan; pg 187; GD 184; Law; mechanics lien

defendant; 1871 Jan; pg 188; GD 200; Law; trespass on the case of premesis, attachment

defendant; 1871 Jan; pg 188; GD 201; Law; attachment

plaintiff; 1871 Jan; pg 189; GD 202; Law; attachment

defendant; 1871 June; pg 222; GD 177; Law; mechanics lien

defendant; 1871 June; pg 222; GD 175; Law; mechanics lien

defendant; 1871 June; pg 223; GD 184; Law; mechanics lien

defendant; 1871 June; pg 223; GD 169; Law; mechanics lien

defendant; 1871 June; pg 224; GD 171; Law; mechanics lien

defendant; 1871 June; pg 224; GD 174; Law; mechanics lien

Cook, Lyman A

defendant; 1871 Jan; pg 189; GD 203; Law; trespass on the case of premesis, damages $8000, attachment

Copeland (Loveland & Copeland)

plaintiff; 1868 July; pg 91; GD 92; Law; trespass

plaintiff; 1869 Jan; pg 107; GD 92; [Law]; assumpsit

plaintiff; 1870 Jan; pg 159; GD 180; Law; appeal

Copeland, Samuel

defendant; 1867 Mar; pg 14; Law; replevin

defendant; 1868 July; pg 90; GD 91; Law; attachment

plaintiff; 1868 July; pg 91; GD 92; Law; trespass

plaintiff; 1868 Mar; pg 76; GD 83; Law; effectment

defendant; 1869 Jan; pg 106; GD 91; [Law]; attachment

plaintiff; 1869 Jan; pg 107; GD 92; [Law]; assumpsit

plaintiff; 1870 Jan; pg 159; GD 180; Law; appeal

Corson, William

Master in Chancery; 1868 Mar; pg 77; GD 62; Chancery; foreclosure of mortgage

Corson, William A

defendant; [1868 July]; pg 93; GD 97; Law; trespass

defendant; [1868 July]; pg 93; GD 96; Law; trespass

defendant; 1868 July; pg 92; GD 95; Law; trespass

defendant; 1868 July; pg 94; GD 98; Law; trespass

defendant; 1868 July; pg 94; GD 99; Law; trespass

defendant; 1868 July; pg 95; GD 101; Law; trespass

defendant; 1868 July; pg 95; GD 100; Law; trespass

defendant; 1868 July; pg 96; GD 102; Law; trespass

defendant; 1868 July; pg 96; GD 103; Law; [trespass]

defendant; 1868 July; pg 97; GD 104; Law; trespass

defendant; 1868 Mar; pg 87; GD 79; Law; trespass

defendant; 1868 Mar; pg 87; GD 78; Law; trespass

defendant; 1868 Mar; pg 88; GD 80; Law; trespass

defendant; 1869 Jan; pg 105; GD 78; [Law]; trespass, $5000 damages

defendant; 1869 Jan; pg 108; GD 98; [Law]; trespass, $5000 damages

defendant; 1869 July; pg 117; GD 78; Law; trespass, $5000 damages

defendant; 1869 July; pg 118; GD 99; Law; trespass, $5000 damages

defendant; 1869 July; pg 130; GD 149; Law; replevin

plaintiff; 1871 Jan; pg 193; GD 217; Law; appeal

Cort, Henry W

defendant; 1871 June; pg 230; GD 275; Law; assumpsit

Coulson, Charles M

defendant; 1872 Jan; pg 261; GD 301; Law; mechanics lien

Coulson, Clarisia [Clarissa] A

defendant; 1871 Jan; pg 201; GD 211; Chancery; foreclosure of mortgage

Coulson, William W

defendant; 1869 July; pg 125; GD 138; Law; mechanics lien

defendant; 1870 Jan; pg 145; GD 138; Law; mechanics lien

Coulson, Wm W

defendant; 1871 Jan; pg 180; GD 138; Law; mechanics lien

defendant; 1871 Jan; pg 201; GD 211; Chancery; foreclosure of mortgage

Couray [Conoy], Thomas

defendant; 1870 Jan; pg 163; GD 135; Chancery; foreclosure

Cranmer, J J

defendant; 1872 Jan; pg 260; GD 299; Law; assumpsit, damage, $1200

appraiser; 1872 Jan; pg 269; GD 305; Chancery; demands

Cranmer, Johnathan [Jonathan] J
  defendant; 1871 June; pg 229; GD 272; Law; assumpsit, damages $1000
  defendant; 1872 Jan; pg 253; GD 272; Law; assumpsit, damages $1000

Crawford, E D
  plaintiff; 1868 Mar; pg 73; GD 77; Law; appellant

Cressey (Cushman & Cressey)
  defendant; 1869 Jan; pg 105; GD 46; [Law]; mechanics lien
  defendant; 1869 Jan; pg 111; GD 60; [Law]; mechanics lien
  defendant; 1869 July; pg 117; GD 46; Law; mechanics lien
  defendant; 1869 July; pg 119; GD 60; Law; mechanics lien

Cressey, Levi
  defendant; [1872 Jan]; pg 319; GD 60; Law; mechanics lien
  defendant; 1867 Nov; pg 47; GD 46; Law; mechanic lien
  defendant; 1868 July; pg 84; GD 60; Law; mechanic lien
  defendant; 1868 Mar; pg 64; GD 46; Law; mechanic lien
  defendant; 1869 Jan; pg 105; GD 46; [Law]; mechanics lien
  defendant; 1869 Jan; pg 111; GD 60; [Law]; mechanics lien
  defendant; 1869 July; pg 117; GD 46; Law; mechanics lien
  defendant; 1869 July; pg 119; GD 60; Law; mechanics lien

Cressman, Daniel H
  plaintiff; 1870 Jan; pg 157; GD 177; Law; mechanics lien
  plaintiff; 1870 Jan; pg 158; GD 178; Law; attachment
  plaintiff; 1871 Jan; pg 186; GD 178; Law; attachment
  plaintiff; 1871 Jan; pg 186; GD 177; Law; mechanics lien
  plaintiff; 1871 June; pg 222; GD 177; Law; mechanics lien

Cressy (Cushman, Cressy & Company)
  defendant; [1872 Jan]; pg 319; GD 60; Law; mechanics lien

Crocker
  attorney for defendant; 1868 Mar; pg 62; GD 29; Law; trespass
  attorney for plaintiff; 1868 Mar; pg 73; GD 78; Law; trespass
  attorney for plaintiff; 1868 Mar; pg 75; GD 81; Law; trespass
  attorney for plaintiff; 1868 Mar; pg 75; GD 82; Law; effectment
  attorney for plaintiff; 1868 Mar; pg 77; GD 62; Chancery; foreclosure of mortgage

Crosby, Augustine B
  defendant; 1870 Jan; pg 151; GD 165; Law; attachment
  defendant; 1870 Jan; pg 161; GD 184; Law; mechanics lien
  defendant; 1871 Jan; pg 187; GD 184; Law; mechanics lien
  defendant; 1871 Jan; pg 188; GD 201; Law; attachment
  defendant; 1871 Jan; pg 188; GD 200; Law; trespass on the case of premesis, attachment

Crosby, Augustine B, cont.

plaintiff; 1871 Jan; pg 189; GD 202; Law; attachment

defendant; 1871 Jan; pg 189; GD 203; Law; trespass on the case of premesis, damages $8000, attachment

defendant; 1871 June; pg 223; GD 184; Law; mechanics lien

Crosby, Charles H

defendant; 1871 Jan; pg 187; GD 184; Law; mechanics lien

defendant; 1871 Jan; pg 189; GD 203; Law; trespass on the case of premesis, damages $8000, attachment

defendant; 1871 June; pg 223; GD 184; Law; mechanics lien

Crosby, Chas H

defendant; 1870 Jan; pg 161; GD 184; Law; mechanics lien

Culver, Cary

defendant; 1867 Mar; pg 8; Law; replevin

defendant; 1867 Nov; pg 41; GD 14; Law; replevin

defendant; 1867 Nov; pg 42; GD 14; Law; replevin appeal

defendant; 1868 Mar; pg 62; GD 14; Law; replevin

Culver, Robert

plaintiff; 1869 Jan; pg 110; GD 120; [Law]; appeal

defendant; 1871 June; pg 217; GD 250; Law; debt $3000, damages $3000

defendant; 1872 Jan; pg 250; GD 250; Law; debt $3000, damages $3000

Cushman & Cressey

defendant; 1869 Jan; pg 105; GD 46; [Law]; mechanics lien

defendant; 1869 Jan; pg 111; GD 60; [Law]; mechanics lien

defendant; 1869 July; pg 117; GD 46; Law; mechanics lien

defendant; 1869 July; pg 119; GD 60; Law; mechanics lien

Cushman, Alfred

defendant; 1867 Nov; pg 38; GD 40; Criminal; indictment for defacing brand

defendant; 1867 Nov; pg 39; GD 43; Criminal; indictment for larceny

Cushman, Cressy & Company

defendant; [1872 Jan]; pg 319; GD 60; Law; mechanics lien

Cushman, Samuel

defendant; [1872 Jan]; pg 319; GD 60; Law; mechanics lien

defendant; 1867 Nov; pg 47; GD 46; Law; mechanic lien

defendant; 1867 Nov; pg 54; GD 60; Law; mechanic lien

defendant; 1868 July; pg 84; GD 60; Law; mechanic lien

defendant; 1868 Mar; pg 64; GD 46; Law; mechanic lien

defendant; 1868 Mar; pg 68; GD 60; Law; mechanic lien

defendant; 1869 Jan; pg 105; GD 46; [Law]; mechanics lien

defendant; 1869 Jan; pg 111; GD 60; [Law]; mechanics lien

defendant; 1869 July; pg 117; GD 46; Law; mechanics lien

Davis (Finch & Davis)

defendant; 1871 Jan; pg 194; GD 218; Law; mechanics lien

defendant; 1871 Jan; pg 194; GD 219; Law; mechanics lien

defendant; 1871 June; pg 220; GD 218; Law; mechanics lien

defendant; 1871 June; pg 221; GD 219; Law; mechanics lien

defendant; 1872 Jan; pg 249; GD 218; Law; mechanics lien

defendant; 1872 Jan; pg 250; GD 219; Law; mechanics lien

Davis, John

plaintiff; 1872 Jan; pg 262; GD 302; Law; mechanics lien

Davis, Joseph

defendant; 1871 Jan; pg 194; GD 219; Law; mechanics lien

defendant; 1871 Jan; pg 194; GD 218; Law; mechanics lien

defendant; 1871 June; pg 220; GD 218; Law; mechanics lien

defendant; 1871 June; pg 221; GD 219; Law; mechanics lien

defendant; 1872 Jan; pg 249; GD 218; Law; mechanics lien

defendant; 1872 Jan; pg 250; GD 219; Law; mechanics lien

Day, A R

defendant; 1872 Jan; pg 255; GD 281; Law; trespass on the case of premises, damages $2000

Day, Alanson R

defendant; 1872 Jan; pg 258; GD 293; Law; action of debt, $10,000, damages $3,500

DeBacker, John

defendant; 1867 Mar; pg 31; Law; trespass

defendant; 1867 Mar; pg 5; Law; appeal

defendant; 1867 Nov; pg 47; GD 39; Law; trespass

defendant; 1871 June; pg 216; GD 271; Criminal; to keep the peace

defendant; 1871 June; pg 229; GD 269; Law; appeal

defendant; 1872 Jan; pg 249; GD 269; Law; appeal

Decker

attorney for plaintiff; 1867 Nov; pg 42; GD 14; Law; replevin appeal

attorney for defendant; 1867 Nov; pg 45; GD 36; Law; assumpsit

attorney for plaintiff; 1867 Nov; pg 46; GD 35; Law; assumpsit

attorney for defendant; 1867 Nov; pg 51; GD 53; Law; attachment

attorney for defendant; 1868 July; pg 91; GD 93; Law; trespass

attorney for plaintiff; 1868 Mar; pg 62; GD 14; Law; replevin

attorney for defendant; 1868 Mar; pg 66; GD 53; Law; attachment

attorney for defendant; 1868 Mar; pg 73; GD 78; Law; trespass

attorney for defendant; 1868 Mar; pg 75; GD 81; Law; trespass

attorney for defendant; 1868 Mar; pg 75; GD 82; Law; effectment

attorney for defendant; 1869 Jan; pg 107; GD 92; [Law]; assumpsit

attorney for plaintiff; 1869 Jan; pg 112; GD 111; Chancery; divorce

Decker, J H, cont.
defendant; 1872 Jan; pg 263; GD 212; Chancery; bill for exceeding their authority and other illegal proceedings
attorney for plaintiff; 1872 Jan; pg 270; GD 306; Chancery; application to appoint appraisers
defendant; 1871 Jan; pg 202; GD 212; Chancery; bill for exceeding their authority and other illegal proceedings

Decker, Jas H
defendant; 1871 June; pg 232; GD 212; Chancery; bill for exceeding their authority and other illegal proceedings

Delahunt, Daniel
plaintiff; 1867 Mar; pg 23; Law; trespass
plaintiff; 1867 Nov; pg 44; GD 30; Law; trespass at issue
plaintiff; 1868 Mar; pg 63; GD 30; Law; trespass

Denver and Boulder Valley Railway and Telegraph Extention Company
plaintiff; 1872 Jan; pg 270; GD 306; Chancery; application to appoint appraisers

Dickens, William H
defendant; 1869 July; pg 125; GD 137; Law; action debt $1000, damages $1000
defendant; 1870 Jan; pg 145; GD 137; Law; action debt $1000, damages $1000

defendant; 1871 Jan; pg 179; GD 137; Law; motion of debt $1000, damages $1000
defendant; 1871 June; pg 227; GD 137; Law; actions of debt, damages $1000
defendant; 1872 Jan; pg 253; GD 137; Law; action of debt, damages $100

Donald, Charles
defendant; 1867 Mar; pg 25; Law; appeal
defendant; 1867 Nov; pg 45; GD 32; Law; appeal

Donnelly, Edward
defendant; 1870 Jan; pg 142; GD 156; Criminal; indictment for selling liquor without license
plaintiff; 1870 Jan; pg 149; GD 161; Law; attachment
plaintiff; 1870 Jan; pg 161; GD 185; Law; assumpsit, damages $1000

Donnelly, Leo
defendant; 1871 June; pg 212; GD 246; Criminal; indictment for keeping tippling house open on the Sabbath day

Doran, James
defendant; 1871 Jan; pg 190; GD 206; Law; appeal

Dougherty, Lewis D
plaintiff; 1868 July; pg 95; GD 101; Law; trespass

Doughterty, Lewis
defendant; 1868 Mar; pg 78; GD 84; Criminal; indictment for resisting officer

Douty, Andrew
defendant; 1867 Nov; pg 53; GD
58; Law; assumpsit
defendant; 1868 Mar; pg 68; GD
58; Law; assumpsit

Douty, Sylvester
defendant; 1867 Nov; pg 53; GD
58; Law; assumpsit
defendant; 1868 Mar; pg 68; GD
58; Law; assumpsit

Dubois, James E
defendant; 1867 Nov; pg 40; GD
44; Criminal; indictment for
larceny

Dubois, William
defendant; 1867 Nov; pg 40; GD
44; Criminal; indictment for
larceny

Dunagan, Jackson J
plaintiff; 1872 Jan; pg 260; GD 298;
Law; assumpsit, damages $300

Duncan, John
plaintiff; 1869 July; pg 127; GD
143; Law; replevin

Dunston, Edward
defendant; 1867 Nov; pg 53; GD
59; Law; attachment

Dunston, Thomas
defendant; 1867 Nov; pg 53; GD
59; Law; attachment

Dwight, Jason L
plaintiff; 1871 Jan; pg 194; GD
218; Law; mechanics lien
plaintiff; 1871 June; pg 220; GD
218; Law; mechanics lien
plaintiff; 1872 Jan; pg 249; GD
218; Law; mechanics lien

E

E T Wells & Brown
attorney for plaintiff; 1871 Jan; pg
197; GD 226; Law; assumpsit

Earnest, Fletcher
defendant; 1867 Nov; pg 51; GD
54; Law; mechanic lien
defendant; 1868 July; pg 83; GD
54; Law; mechanic lien
defendant; 1868 Mar; pg 67; GD
54; Law; mechanic lien

Edson, William
alias of Henry Fowler; 1871 June;
pg 234; GD 256; Chancery;
divorce

Elbert (Charles & Elbert)
attorney for plaintiff; 1872 Jan; pg
255; GD 281; Law; trespass on
the case of premises, damages
$2000

Elder, Clarence P
plaintiff; 1868 Mar; pg 75; GD 82;
Law; effectment
plaintiff; 1868 Mar; pg 75; GD 81;
Law; trespass
plaintiff; 1868 Mar; pg 88; GD 81;
Law; trespass
plaintiff; 1869 Jan; pg 106; GD 81;
[Law]; trespass, $1000 damages
plaintiff; 1869 July; pg 118; GD 81;
Law; trespass, $10,000 damages

Elems, Richard
plaintiff; 1869 July; pg 123; GD
128; Law; mechanics lien
plaintiff; 1870 Jan; pg 144; GD
128; Law; mechanics lien

Elems, Richard, cont.

plaintiff; 1871 Jan; pg 179; GD 128; Law; mechanics lien

plaintiff; 1871 June; pg 218; GD 128; Law; mechanics lien

defendant; 1872 Jan; pg 247; GD 128; Law; mechanics lien

defendant; 1872 Jan; pg 265; GD 291; Chancery; writ of injunction

Ellingham & Brother

plaintiff; 1870 Jan; pg 143; GD 126; Law; mechanics lien

Ellingham Brothers

plaintiff; 1869 July; pg 122; GD 126; Law; mechanics lien

plaintiff; 1871 Jan; pg 178; GD 126; Law; mechanics lien

plaintiff; 1871 June; pg 218; GD 126; Law; mechanics lien

plaintiff; 1872 Jan; pg 247; GD 126; Law; mechanics lien

Ellingham, John

plaintiff; 1869 July; pg 122; GD 126; Law; mechanics lien

plaintiff; 1870 Jan; pg 143; GD 126; Law; mechanics lien

plaintiff; 1871 June; pg 218; GD 126; Law; mechanics lien

plaintiff; 1872 Jan; pg 247; GD 126; Law; mechanics lien

defendant; 1872 Jan; pg 265; GD 291; Chancery; writ of injunction

Ellingham, Robert

plaintiff; 1869 July; pg 122; GD 126; Law; mechanics lien

plaintiff; 1870 Jan; pg 143; GD 126; Law; mechanics lien

plaintiff; 1871 Jan; pg 178; GD 126; Law; mechanics lien

plaintiff; 1871 Jan; pg 178; GD 126; Law; mechanics lien

plaintiff; 1871 June; pg 218; GD 126; Law; mechanics lien

plaintiff; 1872 Jan; pg 247; GD 126; Law; mechanics lien

defendant; 1872 Jan; pg 265; GD 291; Chancery; writ of injunction

Ellingham, Rob

appraiser; 1872 Jan; pg 269; GD 305; Chancery; demands

Emerson, Charles

defendant; 1872 Jan; pg 261; GD 301; Law; mechanics lien

Evans, David

plaintiff; 1868 July; pg 97; GD 104; Law; trespass

Eystin, C S

Judge [?]; 1868 Mar; pg 63; GD 36; Law; assumpsit

F

Fall, Arnold

plaintiff; 1871 Jan; pg 195; GD 220; Law; appeal

Fall, Gustavus

plaintiff; 1871 Jan; pg 195; GD 220; Law; appeal

Farrar, Decatur

defendant; 1869 July; pg 125; GD 138; Law; mechanics lien

defendant; 1870 Jan; pg 145; GD 138; Law; mechanics lien

defendant; 1871 Jan; pg 200; GD
204; Chancery; foreclosure of
mortgage

defendant; 1871 Jan; pg 180; GD
138; Law; mechanics lien

Ferguson, Mary
plaintiff; 1867 Mar; pg 34; Chancery; divorce

Ferguson, Moses
defendant; 1867 Mar; pg 34; Chancery; divorce

Finch & Davis
defendant; 1871 Jan; pg 194; GD
218; Law; mechanics lien
defendant; 1871 Jan; pg 194; GD
219; Law; mechanics lien
defendant; 1871 June; pg 220; GD
218; Law; mechanics lien
defendant; 1871 June; pg 221; GD
219; Law; mechanics lien
defendant; 1872 Jan; pg 249; GD
218; Law; mechanics lien
defendant; 1872 Jan; pg 250; GD
219; Law; mechanics lien

Finch, John B
defendant; 1871 June; pg 216; GD
277; Criminal; indictment for
assault with intent to murder

Finch, William
defendant; 1871 Jan; pg 194; GD
219; Law; mechanics lien
defendant; 1871 Jan; pg 194; GD
218; Law; mechanics lien
defendant; 1871 June; pg 220; GD
218; Law; mechanics lien
defendant; 1871 June; pg 221; GD
219; Law; mechanics lien

defendant; 1872 Jan; pg 249; GD
218; Law; mechanics lien
defendant; 1872 Jan; pg 250; GD
219; Law; mechanics lien

Fonda, Giles H
defendant; 1871 June; pg 210; GD
243; Criminal; indictment for
keeping a gambling house

Foote, James B
defendant; 1867 Mar; pg 20; Law;
replevin
defendant; 1867 Nov; pg 43; GD
27; Law; replevin

Ford, John B
defendant; 1872 Jan; pg 243; GD
277; Criminal; indictment for
assault with intent to kill

Fowler, Henry
defendant; 1871 June; pg 234; GD
256; Chancery; divorce

Fowler, Mary E
plaintiff; 1871 June; pg 234; GD
256; Chancery; divorce

Fowler, William B
plaintiff; 1870 Jan; pg 161; GD
184; Law; mechanics lien
plaintiff; 1871 Jan; pg 187; GD
184; Law; mechanics lien
plaintiff; 1871 June; pg 223; GD
184; Law; mechanics lien

France
attorney for defendant; 1868 July;
pg 97; GD 105; Law; assumpsit
attorney for defendant; 1871 Jan;
pg 191; GD 213; Law; trespass
damages $1000

Francis, Joseph
defendant; 1871 Jan; pg 205; GD 234; Law; appeal, change of venue from Gilpin County

Froggett, Edward
defendant; 1867 Mar; pg 26; Law; appeal
plaintiff; 1867 Mar; pg 33; Chancery; divorce
plaintiff; 1867 Nov; pg 55; GD 11; Chancery; divorce

Froggett, Jane
defendant; 1867 Mar; pg 33; Chancery; divorce
defendant; 1867 Nov; pg 55; GD 11; Chancery; divorce

Frost, Mary A
defendant; 1870 Jan; pg 164; GD 134; Chancery; chancery
defendant; 1871 Jan; pg 204; GD 134; Chancery
Fry, William H
defendant; 1869 Jan; pg 111; GD 114; [Law]; appeal

G

Gafton, William
plaintiff; 1867 Mar; pg 30; Law; assumpsit

Gardener, Isaac A
defendant; 1868 Mar; pg 70; GD 72; Law; debt

Gardner, Dyre N
plaintiff; 1871 June; pg 236; GD 268; Chancery; a writ of injunction

plaintiff; 1872 Jan; pg 265; GD 268; Chancery; writ of injunction

Geer, Charles
defendant; 1868 July; pg 100; GD 108; Law [Criminal]; indictment for larceny
defendant; 1869 Jan; pg 103; GD 108; Criminal; indictment for larceny
defendant; 1869 July; pg 116; GD 108; Criminal; larceny
defendant; 1870 Jan; pg 139; GD 108; Criminal; indictment for malicious mischief

Geer, Solomon
defendant; 1868 July; pg 100; GD 109; Law [Criminal]; indictment for malicious mischief

Gifford, Abraham
defendant; 1868 July; pg 89; GD 88; Law; trespass

Gile, Joseph
defendant; 1869 July; pg 120; GD 29; Law; assumpsit

Gile, Joseph F
defendant; 1867 Mar; pg 22; Law; trespass
defendant; 1867 Nov; pg 43; GD 29; Law; trespass
defendant; 1868 Mar; pg 62; GD 29; Law; trespass

Goodwin, Harrison
plaintiff; 1867 Mar; pg 7; Law; replevin
plaintiff; 1867 Nov; pg 48; GD 47; Law; debt
plaintiff; 1867 Nov; pg 54; GD 9; Law; replevin, at issue

plaintiff; 1868 Mar; pg 65; GD 47; Law; debt

Gorsline
Judge; 1867 Mar; pg 16; Law; appeal from the county commissioners

Goss, John W
plaintiff; 1871 Jan; pg 195; GD 221; Law; appeal

Gould, Jotham
defendant; 1869 July; pg 126; GD 139; Law; assumpsit, damages $1000

Gould, Selsana
defendant; 1867 Mar; pg 36; Chancery; injunction and trespass

Gould, W H
defendant; 1867 Mar; pg 36; Chancery; injunction and trespass

Gouldman, Elias
plaintiff; 1871 Jan; pg 195; GD 220; Law; appeal

Grafton, William
plaintiff; 1867 Nov; pg 46; GD 35; Law; assumpsit

Graham, Hurcles [Hercules]
plaintiff; 1870 Jan; pg 153; GD 168; Law; appeal

Graham, Samuel
defendant; 1872 Jan; pg 255; GD 282; Law; appeal
plaintiff; 1872 Jan; pg 262; GD 302; Law; mechanics lien

Graham, Thomas J
defendant; 1869 July; pg 135; GD 133; Chancery; foreclosure of mortgage

defendant; 1871 Jan; pg 199; GD 133; Chancery; foreclosure of mortgage
plaintiff; 1871 Jan; pg 202; GD 212; Chancery; bill for exceeding their authority and other illegal proceedings
defendant; 1871 June; pg 228; GD 267; Law; trespass on premesis, damages $3000, suit withdrawn by plaintiff
plaintiff; 1871 June; pg 232; GD 212; Chancery; bill for exceeding their authority and other illegal proceedings
plaintiff; 1872 Jan; pg 263; GD 212; Chancery; bill for exceeding their authority and other illegal proceedings

Graham, Thos J
defendant; 1870 Jan; pg 162; GD 133; Chancery; foreclosure

Green, Henry
defendant; [1868 July]; pg 93; GD 97; Law; trespass
defendant; [1868 July]; pg 93; GD 96; Law; trespass
defendant; 1868 July; pg 92; GD 95; Law; trespass
defendant; 1868 July; pg 94; GD 99; Law; trespass
defendant; 1868 July; pg 94; GD 98; Law; trespass
defendant; 1868 July; pg 95; GD 101; Law; trespass
defendant; 1868 July; pg 95; GD 100; Law; trespass
defendant; 1868 July; pg 96; GD 102; Law; trespass

Green, Henry, cont.

defendant; 1868 July; pg 96; GD 103; Law; [trespass]

defendant; 1868 July; pg 97; GD 104; Law; trespass

defendant; 1868 Mar; pg 73; GD 78; Law; trespass

defendant; 1868 Mar; pg 74; GD 80; Law; trespass

defendant; 1868 Mar; pg 74; GD 79; Law; trespass

defendant; 1868 Mar; pg 87; GD 78; Law; trespass

defendant; 1868 Mar; pg 87; GD 79; Law; trespass

defendant; 1868 Mar; pg 88; GD 80; Law; trespass

defendant; 1869 Jan; pg 105; GD 78; [Law]; trespass, $5000 damages

defendant; 1869 Jan; pg 108; GD 98; [Law]; trespass, $5000 damages

defendant; 1869 Jan; pg 109; GD 118; [Law]; debt $1000, damages $5000

defendant; 1869 July; pg 117; GD 78; Law; trespass, $5000 damages

defendant; 1869 July; pg 118; GD 99; Law; trespass, $5000 damages

defendant; 1869 July; pg 127; GD 143; Law; replevin

defendant; 1869 July; pg 130; GD 148; Law; debt $1000, damages $5000

defendant; 1870 Jan; pg 147; GD 148; Law; debt $1000, damages $5000

Green, Stephen H

defendant; 1867 Mar; pg 21; Law; assumpsit

Griswold (J A & H F Griswold)

plaintiff; 1871 June; pg 225; GD 258; Law; assumpsit, damages $2000

Griswold, Henry F

plaintiff; 1871 June; pg 225; GD 258; Law; assumpsit, damages $2000

Griswold, Joseph A

plaintiff; 1871 June; pg 225; GD 258; Law; assumpsit, damages $2000

Guilfoyle, Cornelius

plaintiff; 1869 July; pg 131; GD 150; Law; mechanics lien

plaintiff; 1870 Jan; pg 147; GD 150; Law; mechanics lien

plaintiff; 1871 Jan; pg 181; GD 150; Law; mechanics lien

plaintiff; 1871 June; pg 219; GD 150; Law; mechanics lien

plaintiff; 1872 Jan; pg 246; GD 150; Law; mechanics lien

defendant; 1872 Jan; pg 265; GD 291; Chancery; writ of injunction

Gwin [Guin], Thos

appraiser; 1872 Jan; pg 270; GD 306; Chancery; application to appoint appraisers

H

Harris, Jesse
  defendant; 1867 Nov; pg 37; Criminal; indictment for murder
  defendant; 1868 July; pg 101; GD 110; Criminal; indictment for murder
  defendant; 1868 July; pg 80; GD 2; Criminal; indictment for murder
  defendant; 1868 Mar; pg 59; GD 2; Criminal; indictment for murder
  defendant; 1869 Jan; pg 103; GD 110; Criminal; indictment for murder
  defendant; 1869 July; pg 116; GD 110; Criminal; murder
  defendant; 1870 Jan; pg 141; GD 110; Criminal; indictment for murder
  defendant; 1871 Jan; pg 171; GD 110; Criminal; indictment for murder
  defendant; 1871 June; pg 206; GD 110; Criminal; indictment for murder

Harris, Jessie [Jesse]
  defendant; 1867 Mar; pg 1; Criminal; indictment for murder

Harris, John
  defendant; 1870 Jan; pg 148; GD 159; Law; attachment

Harris, John P
  defendant; 1870 Jan; pg 149; GD 161; Law; attachment
  defendant; 1870 Jan; pg 150; GD 163; Law; attachment
  defendant; 1870 Jan; pg 150; GD 162; Law; attachment

Harrison (Brown, Harrison & Putman)
  attorney for plaintiff; 1871 Jan; pg 192; GD 214; Law; debt, damages $300
  attorney for plaintiff; 1871 Jan; pg 193; GD 216; Law; plea of debt, damages $700

Haus, William W
  defendant; 1867 Nov; pg 49; GD 51; Law; appeal

Hayden, Samuel
  defendant; 1867 Mar; pg 4; Law; appeal
  defendant; 1867 Nov; pg 41; GD 6; Law; appeal
  defendant; 1867 Nov; pg 42; GD 6; Law; appeal at issue
  defendant; 1870 Jan; pg 158; GD 179; Law; replevin

Hayes, Martin B
  plaintiff; 1871 Jan; pg 197; GD 226; Law; assumpsit

Hays, Samuel M
  defendant; 1872 Jan; pg 256; GD 288; Law; assumpsit, damages $1500

Healey & Holt
  plaintiff; 1867 Mar; pg 14; Law; replevin
  plaintiff; 1867 Mar; pg 15; Law; assumpsit

Henry (Pomeroy & Henry)
  defendant; 1872 Jan; pg 259; GD 296; Law; assumpsit, debt $2000

Henry, Oren H
  defendant; 1871 Jan; pg 205; GD 233; Law; appeal

Henry, Ormal E
  defendant; 1871 Jan; pg 205; GD
    233; Law; appeal
  defendant; 1872 Jan; pg 259; GD
    296; Law; assumpsit, debt $2000

Heredge, Walter
  defendant; 1867 Nov; pg 40; GD
    45; Criminal; indictment for
    larceny
  defendant; 1868 July; pg 80; GD
    45; Criminal; indictment for
    larceny

Hesler, John
  plaintiff; 1868 July; pg 94; GD 99;
    Law; trespass
  plaintiff; 1869 Jan; pg 108; GD 98;
    [Law]; trespass, $5000 damages
  plaintiff; 1869 July; pg 118; GD 99;
    Law; trespass, $5000 damages

Hewes, John M
  defendant; [1868 July]; pg 93; GD
    96; Law; trespass
  defendant; [1868 July]; pg 93; GD
    97; Law; trespass
  plaintiff; 1867 Mar; pg 8; Law;
    replevin
  plaintiff; 1867 Nov; pg 41; GD 14;
    Law; replevin
  plaintiff; 1867 Nov; pg 42; GD 14;
    Law; replevin appeal
  plaintiff; 1868 July; pg 90; GD 91;
    Law; attachment
  defendant; 1868 July; pg 91; GD
    93; Law; trespass
  defendant; 1868 July; pg 91; GD
    92; Law; trespass
  defendant; 1868 July; pg 92; GD
    95; Law; trespass
  defendant; 1868 July; pg 94; GD
    98; Law; trespass
  defendant; 1868 July; pg 94; GD
    99; Law; trespass
  defendant; 1868 July; pg 95; GD
    100; Law; trespass
  defendant; 1868 July; pg 95; GD
    101; Law; trespass
  defendant; 1868 July; pg 96; GD
    103; Law; [trespass]
  defendant; 1868 July; pg 96; GD
    102; Law; trespass
  defendant; 1868 July; pg 97; GD
    104; Law; trespass
  plaintiff; 1868 Mar; pg 62; GD 14;
    Law; replevin
  defendant; 1868 Mar; pg 87; GD
    79; Law; trespass
  defendant; 1868 Mar; pg 87; GD
    78; Law; trespass
  defendant; 1868 Mar; pg 88; GD
    80; Law; trespass
  defendant; 1869 Jan; pg 105; GD
    78; [Law]; trespass, $5000 dam-
    ages
  plaintiff; 1869 Jan; pg 106; GD 91;
    [Law]; attachment
  defendant; 1869 Jan; pg 107; GD
    92; [Law]; assumpsit
  defendant; 1869 Jan; pg 108; GD
    98; [Law]; trespass, $5000 dam-
    ages
  defendant; 1869 July; pg 117; GD
    78; Law; trespass, $5000 dam-
    ages
  defendant; 1869 July; pg 118; GD
    99; Law; trespass, $5000 dam-
    ages
  defendant; 1870 Jan; pg 160; GD
    183; Law; assumpsit

Hickes [Hicks], J M
defendant; 1868 Mar; pg 73; GD
77; Law; appellant

Hickes [Hicks], Jacob
defendant; 1868 July; pg 85; GD
70; Law; assumpsit
defendant; 1868 Mar; pg 69; GD
70; Law; assumpsit

Hicks, Jacob M
defendant; 1867 Nov; pg 49; GD
51; Law; appeal

Hinman, P M
plaintiff; 1872 Jan; pg 262; GD
301; Law; appeal

Hollingsworth, J B
plaintiff; 1867 Mar; pg 17; Law;
appeal by certiorari
defendant; 1869 Jan; pg 102; GD
67; Criminal; indictment for
obstructing high way

Hollingsworth, John
defendant; 1868 July; pg 81; GD
86; Criminal; indictment for
obstructing public highway
defendant; 1868 Mar; pg 78; GD
86; Criminal; indictment for
obstructing public hyway

Holt (Healy & Holt)
plaintiff; 1867 Mar; pg 14; Law;
replevin
plaintiff; 1867 Mar; pg 14; Law;
replevin

Holt, George C
plaintiff; 1869 Jan; pg 109; GD
119; [Law]; assumpsit

Hook, Charles H
defendant; 1871 Jan; pg 175; GD
198; Criminal; indictment for
keeping open a tippling house
on the Sabbath day
defendant; 1871 Jan; pg 175; GD
197; Criminal; indictment for
keeping a building and room to
be used for gambling

Hopkins, Wm L
defendant; 1871 Jan; pg 193; GD
217; Law; appeal

Horner, J W
attorney for plaintiff; 1871 June;
pg 225; GD 258; Law; assumpsit,
damages $2000
attorney for plaintiff; 1871 June;
pg 225; GD 259; Law; assumpsit,
damages $2000
attorney for plaintiff; 1872 Jan; pg
268; GD 286; Chancery; divorce

Horton, Wm R
notice given; 1870 Jan; pg 161; GD
184; Law; mechanics lien
defendant; 1871 Jan; pg 187; GD
184; Law; mechanics lien
defendant; 1871 June; pg 223; GD
184; Law; mechanics lien

Housel, Peter M
defendant; 1867 Mar; pg 31; Law;
trespass
defendant; 1867 Mar; pg 5; Law;
appeal
defendant; 1867 Nov; pg 47; GD
39; Law; trespass

Howard, Nephi M
defendant; 1867 Nov; pg 50; GD
52; Law; replevin

defendant; 1871 Jan; pg 192; GD 214; Law; debt, damages $300

Howard, Norman R
defendant; 1871 Jan; pg 192; GD 214; Law; debt, damages $300

Hoyt, David
plaintiff; 1867 Nov; pg 56; GD 62; Chancery; foreclosure of mortgage
plaintiff; 1868 Mar; pg 77; GD 62; Chancery; foreclosure of mortgage

Hubbard, Horace W
defendant; [1868 July]; pg 93; GD 96; Law; trespass
defendant; [1868 July]; pg 93; GD 97; Law; trespass
defendant; 1868 July; pg 92; GD 95; Law; trespass
defendant; 1868 July; pg 94; GD 98; Law; trespass
defendant; 1868 July; pg 94; GD 99; Law; trespass
defendant; 1868 July; pg 95; GD 101; Law; trespass
defendant; 1868 July; pg 95; GD 100; Law; trespass
defendant; 1868 July; pg 96; GD 102; Law; trespass
defendant; 1868 July; pg 96; GD 103; Law; [trespass]
defendant; 1868 July; pg 97; GD 104; Law; trespass
defendant; 1868 Mar; pg 87; GD 79; Law; trespass
defendant; 1868 Mar; pg 87; GD 78; Law; trespass
defendant; 1868 Mar; pg 88; GD 80; Law; trespass

defendant; 1869 Jan; pg 105; GD 78; [Law]; trespass, $5000 damages
defendant; 1869 Jan; pg 108; GD 98; [Law]; trespass, $5000 damages
defendant; 1869 July; pg 117; GD 78; Law; trespass, $5000 damages
defendant; 1869 July; pg 118; GD 99; Law; trespass, $5000 damages

Hulling, John M
plaintiff; 1868 Mar; pg 73; GD 78; Law; trespass
defendant; 1868 Mar; pg 78; GD 84; Criminal; indictment for resisting officer
plaintiff; 1868 Mar; pg 87; GD 78; Law; trespass
plaintiff; 1869 Jan; pg 105; GD 78; [Law]; trespass, $5000 damages
plaintiff; 1869 July; pg 117; GD 78; Law; trespass, $5000 damages

Humphrey, Mary M
petitioner; 1872 Jan; pg 266; GD 276; Chancery; Petition of Mary M Humphries, widow &c to sell real estate

Humphries, Mary M
petitioner; 1871 June; pg 237; Chancery; Petition of Mary M Humphries, widow &c to sell real estate

Hunt
attorney for defendant; 1868 Mar; pg 73; GD 78; Law; trespass
attorney for defendant; 1868 Mar; pg 75; GD 82; Law; effectment

Hunt, cont.

attorney for defendant; 1868 Mar; pg 75; GD 81; Law; trespass

Hunt (Browne & Hunt)

attorney for plaintiff; 1867 Nov; pg 48; GD 47; Law

attorney for plaintiff; 1867 Nov; pg 54; GD 9; Law; replevin, at issue

Hussey (Warren Hussey & Co)

plaintiff; 1869 July; pg 125; GD 137; Law; action debt $1000, damages $1000

plaintiff; 1870 Jan; pg 145; GD 137; Law; action debt $1000, damages $1000

plaintiff; 1871 Jan; pg 179; GD 137; Law; motion of debt $1000, damages $1000

plaintiff; 1871 June; pg 227; GD 137; Law; actions of debt, damages $1000

plaintiff; 1872 Jan; pg 253; GD 137; Law; action of debt, damages $100

Hussey, Warren

plaintiff; 1869 July; pg 125; GD 137; Law; action debt $1000, damages $1000

plaintiff; 1870 Jan; pg 145; GD 137; Law; action debt $1000, damages $1000

plaintiff; 1871 Jan; pg 179; GD 137; Law; motion of debt $1000, damages $1000

plaintiff; 1871 June; pg 227; GD 137; Law; actions of debt, damages $1000

plaintiff; 1872 Jan; pg 253; GD 137; Law; action of debt, damages $100

J

J A & H F Griswold

plaintiff; 1871 June; pg 225; GD 258; Law; assumpsit, damages $2000

Jackson, George W

plaintiff; [1868 July]; pg 93; GD 96; Law; trespass

Jackson, L B

defendant; 1867 Nov; pg 52; GD 55; Law; mechanic lien

defendant; 1868 July; pg 83; GD 55; Law; mechanic lien

defendant; 1868 Mar; pg 67; GD 55; Law; mechanic lien

Jacobs, Horatio

defendant; 1869 July; pg 126; GD 141; Law; assumpsit, damage $2000

defendant; 1870 Jan; pg 146; GD 141; Law; assumpsit, damages $2000

Jacobs, Royal

defendant; 1869 July; pg 126; GD 141; Law; assumpsit, damage $2000

defendant; 1870 Jan; pg 146; GD 141; Law; assumpsit, damages $2000

Jay, Mary Jane

plaintiff; 1869 Jan; pg 114; GD 116; [Chancery]; divorce

K

Kelsey, James S
plaintiff; 1871 Jan; pg 205; GD
233; Law; appeal

Kimber, Andrew J
defendant; 1871 Jan; pg 196; GD
225; Law; appeal

Kimberland
attorney for plaintiff; 1867 Nov; pg
47; GD 46; Law
Kinney, Clarissa P
defendant; 1869 July; pg 122; GD
127; Law; appeal
defendant; 1870 Jan; pg 144; GD
127; Law; appeal

Kinney, Edward P
defendant; 1869 July; pg 121; GD
124; Law; appeal
defendant; 1869 July; pg 122; GD
127; Law; appeal
defendant; 1869 July; pg 138; GD
115; Criminal; indictment for
larceny
defendant; 1870 Jan; pg 141; GD
154; Criminal; indictment for
larceny
defendant; 1870 Jan; pg 144; GD
127; Law; appeal
defendant; 1870 Jan; pg 152; GD
166; Law; appeal

Knopple, Charles
defendant; 1867 Mar; pg 1; Criminal; Indictment
defendant; 1867 Nov; pg 37;
Criminal; indictment for assault
with intent to kill

defendant; 1868 Mar; pg 59; GD 1;
Criminal; indictment for assault
with intent to kill

Kohler, Frederick W
defendant; 1869 Jan; pg 109; GD
118; [Law]; debt $1000, damages
$5000
defendant; 1869 July; pg 130; GD
148; Law; debt $1000, damages
$5000
defendant; 1870 Jan; pg 147; GD
148; Law; debt $1000, damages
$5000

L

Lackman, Sally
plaintiff; 1867 Nov; pg 53; GD 58;
Law; assumpsit
plaintiff; 1868 Mar; pg 68; GD 58;
Law; assumpsit

Lamelson, Thomas
defendant; 1869 July; pg 116; GD
110; Criminal; recognizance

Lawson, Charles C
plaintiff; 1868 Mar; pg 71; GD 74;
Law; replevin
plaintiff; 1868 Mar; pg 71; GD 73;
Law; trespass
plaintiff; 1871 June; pg 217; GD
254; Law

Lea, A E
plaintiff; 1868 July; pg 96; GD 102;
Law; trespass

Learnard, Emma C
defendant; 1871 Jan; pg 201; GD
208; Chancery; divorce

Learnard, Horace A
plaintiff; 1871 Jan; pg 201; GD 208; Chancery; divorce

Leyden, Martin
defendant; 1871 Jan; pg 176; GD 208; Criminal; indictment for perjury from Jefferson County

Lickes, John
plaintiff; 1869 July; pg 127; GD 142; Law; attachment

Lin, Jonathan
defendant; 1869 Jan; pg 111; GD 60; [Law]; mechanics lien

Linclaw, Jotham
plaintiff; 1869 July; pg 120; GD 29; Law; assumpsit

Linclow, Jonathan
plaintiff; 1867 Mar; pg 22; Law; trespass
plaintiff; 1867 Nov; pg 43; GD 29; Law; trespass
plaintiff; 1868 Mar; pg 62; GD 29; Law; trespass

Lirast, Mary A
defendant; 1869 July; pg 136; GD 134; Chancery

Lockridge, Charles
defendant; 1867 Nov; pg 39; GD 42; Criminal; malicious mischief

London and Colorado Company
plaintiff; 1872 Jan; pg 261; GD 300; Law; assumpsit, damages $6000
defendant; 1872 Jan; pg 262; GD 302; Law; mechanics lien

Lovejoy, Elijah
defendant; 1867 Nov; pg 54; GD 61; Law; appeal

Loveland & Copeland
plaintiff; 1868 July; pg 91; GD 92; Law; trespass
plaintiff; 1869 Jan; pg 107; GD 92; [Law]; assumpsit
plaintiff; 1870 Jan; pg 159; GD 180; Law; appeal

Loveland, W A H
plaintiff; 1870 Jan; pg 159; GD 180; Law; appeal

Loveland, William A H
plaintiff; 1868 July; pg 91; GD 92; Law; trespass
plaintiff; 1869 Jan; pg 107; GD 92; [Law]; assumpsit

Lowe, Rodger [Roger] S
plaintiff; 1869 July; pg 136; GD 134; Chancery
plaintiff; 1870 Jan; pg 164; GD 134; Chancery; chancery

Lowe, Roger S
defendant; 1871 Jan; pg 190; GD 205; Law; appeal
plaintiff; 1871 Jan; pg 204; GD 134; Chancery

M

Mackey [Macky], Andrew J
plaintiff; 1867 Mar; pg 35; Chancery; foreclosure of mortgage
plaintiff; 1867 Nov; pg 55; GD 13; Chancery; foreclosure of mortgage
plaintiff; 1870 Jan; pg 149; GD 160; Law; replevin

Macky, A J
defendant; 1872 Jan; pg 258; GD 293; Law; action of debt, $10,000, damages $3,500

Macky, Andrew J
plaintiff; 1872 Jan; pg 256; GD 289; Law; assumpsit, damages $400
plaintiff; 1872 Jan; pg 257; GD 290; Law; assumpsit, damages $200

Maddox, James F
defendant; 1871 June; pg 221; GD 227; Law; debt $600, damages $600

Maddox, James J
defendant; 1872 Jan; pg 254; GD 227; Law; debt, $600, damage $600

Maddox, James T
defendant; 1871 Jan; pg 197; GD 227; Law; debt, $600

Maddox, Jemima
plaintiff; 1871 Jan; pg 203; GD 223; Chancery; divorce
plaintiff; 1871 June; pg 232; GD 223; Chancery; bill for divorce and for confirmation of masters sale

Maddox, Peter
defendant; 1871 Jan; pg 203; GD 223; Chancery; divorce
defendant; 1871 June; pg 232; GD 223; Chancery; bill for divorce and for confirmation of masters sale

Mann, William J
defendant; 1871 June; pg 236; GD 268; Chancery; a writ of injunction

defendant; 1872 Jan; pg 265; GD 268; Chancery; writ of injunction

Manners, Harvey
defendant; 1869 July; pg 125; GD 137; Law; action debt $1000, damages $1000
defendant; 1870 Jan; pg 145; GD 137; Law; action debt $1000, damages $1000
defendant; 1871 Jan; pg 179; GD 137; Law; motion of debt $1000, damages $1000
defendant; 1871 June; pg 227; GD 137; Law; actions of debt, damages $1000
defendant; 1872 Jan; pg 253; GD 137; Law; action of debt, damages $100

Manning, William
defendant; [1868 July]; pg 93; GD 96; Law; trespass
defendant; [1868 July]; pg 93; GD 97; Law; trespass
defendant; 1868 July; pg 94; GD 99; Law; trespass
defendant; 1868 July; pg 94; GD 98; Law; trespass
defendant; 1868 July; pg 95; GD 101; Law; trespass
defendant; 1868 July; pg 95; GD 100; Law; trespass
defendant; 1868 July; pg 96; GD 103; Law; [trespass]
defendant; 1868 July; pg 96; GD 102; Law; trespass
defendant; 1868 July; pg 97; GD 104; Law; trespass

Maxwell, James A
plaintiff; 1869 July; pg 130; GD 149; Law; replevin
defendant; 1871 Jan; pg 197; GD 227; Law; debt, $600
defendant; 1871 June; pg 221; GD 227; Law; debt $600, damages $600
defendant; 1872 Jan; pg 254; GD 227; Law; debt, $600, damage $600

Maxwell, James P
defendant; 1871 Jan; pg 197; GD 227; Law; debt, $600
defendant; 1871 June; pg 221; GD 227; Law; debt $600, damages $600
defendant; 1872 Jan; pg 254; GD 227; Law; debt, $600, damage $600

Maxwell, Julia M
defendant; 1872 Jan; pg 268; GD 286; Chancery; divorce

McDunn, William
plaintiff; 1867 Mar; pg 25; Law; appeal
plaintiff; 1867 Nov; pg 45; GD 32; Law; appeal
plaintiff; 1868 Mar; pg 70; GD 72; Law; debt

McGahey, John F
plaintiff; 1871 Jan; pg 194; GD 219; Law; mechanics lien
plaintiff; 1871 June; pg 221; GD 219; Law; mechanics lien
plaintiff; 1872 Jan; pg 250; GD 219; Law; mechanics lien

McGinnis [Meginnes], Daniel
plaintiff; 1868 July; pg 83; GD 55; Law; mechanic lien
plaintiff; 1868 Mar; pg 67; GD 55; Law; mechanic lien

McGowen, George
plaintiff; 1867 Nov; pg 52; GD 57; Law; appeal

McGuinis [Meginnes], Daniel
plaintiff; 1867 Nov; pg 52; GD 55; Law; mechanic lien

McLinn, J
attorney for plaintiff; 1871 Jan; pg 192; GD 215; Law; assumpsit, damages $300

McMahan, John
defendant; 1872 Jan; pg 244; GD 307; Criminal; indictment for assault with intent to murder

Melvin (Wright, Brown & Melvin)
attorney for defendant; 1871 Jan; pg 199; GD 158; Chancery

Merrill, George
defendant; 1871 June; pg 223; GD 184; Law; mechanics lien

Miler, Joseph Jr
defendant; 1868 Mar; pg 71; GD 74; Law; replevin

Miller & Markham
attorney for defendant; 1869 July; pg 133; GD 154; Law; assumpsit
attorney for plaintiff; 1871 Jan; pg 197; GD 227; Law; debt, $600
attorney for plaintiff; 1871 June; pg 221; GD 227; Law; debt $600, damages $600

attorney for plaintiff; 1872 Jan; pg 254; GD 227; Law; debt, $600, damage $600

Miller, D L

defendant; 1867 Mar; pg 20; Law; replevin

defendant; 1867 Nov; pg 43; GD 27; Law; replevin

Miller, John

defendant; 1871 June; pg 209; GD 240; Criminal; indictment for keeping open a tippling house on the Sabbath day

Mills

attorney for defendant; 1871 Jan; pg 179; GD 137; Law; motion of debt $1000, damages $1000

Milner, Joseph

defendant; 1868 Mar; pg 71; GD 73; Law; trespass

Mooney, Michael

plaintiff; 1869 July; pg 121; GD 125; Law; mechanics lien

plaintiff; 1870 Jan; pg 143; GD 125; Law; mechanics lien

plaintiff; 1871 Jan; pg 178; GD 125; Law; mechanics lien

plaintiff; 1871 June; pg 219; GD 126; Law; mechanics lien

plaintiff; 1872 Jan; pg 246; GD 125; Law; mechanics lien

defendant; 1872 Jan; pg 265; GD 291; Chancery; writ of injunction

Moore, Daniel

defendant; 1867 Nov; pg 58; Criminal; information for gambling

defendant; 1868 July; pg 81; GD 67; Criminal; information for gambling

defendant; 1868 Mar; pg 61; GD 67; Criminal; information for gambling

defendant; 1869 Jan; pg 102; GD 67; Criminal; information for gambling

defendant; 1869 July; pg 115; GD 67; Criminal; information for gambling

defendant; 1870 Jan; pg 139; GD 67; Criminal; information for gambling

Morgan (Post & Morgan)

attorney for defendant; 1867 Nov; pg 47; GD 46; Law

attorney for plaintiff; 1867 Nov; pg 52; GD 57; Law; appeal

attorney for plaintiff; 1868 Mar; pg 87; GD 78; Law; trespass

Morgan (Sayre, Post & Morgan)

attorney for plaintiff; [1868 July]; pg 93; GD 96; Law; trespass

attorney for plaintiff; [1868 July]; pg 93; GD 97; Law; trespass

attorney for plaintiff; 1868 July; pg 94; GD 98; Law; trespass

attorney for plaintiff; 1868 July; pg 94; GD 99; Law; trespass

attorney for plaintiff; 1868 July; pg 95; GD 100; Law; trespass

attorney for plaintiff; 1868 July; pg 95; GD 101; Law; trespass

attorney for plaintiff; 1868 July; pg 96; GD 102; Law; trespass

attorney for plaintiff; 1868 July; pg 96; GD 103; Law; [trespass]

Morgan (Sayre, Post & Morgan), cont.

attorney for plaintiff; 1868 July; pg 97; GD 104; Law; trespass

attorney for plaintiff; 1868 Mar; pg 87; GD 79; Law; trespass

attorney for plaintiff; 1868 Mar; pg 88; GD 80; Law; trespass

Morgan, William

defendant; 1867 Mar; pg 32; Chancery; injunction

Morrell [Morrill], Eugene

defendant; 1869 July; pg 136; GD 134; Chancery

Morrill, Eugene

defendant; 1870 Jan; pg 164; GD 134; Chancery; chancery

defendant; 1871 Jan; pg 204; GD 134; Chancery

Morrill, George

defendant; 1871 Jan; pg 187; GD 184; Law; mechanics lien

Morrill, George W

defendant; 1871 Jan; pg 189; GD 203; Law; trespass on the case of premesis, damages $8000, attachment

Morrison (Partridge & Morrison)

plaintiff; 1869 Jan; pg 109; GD 118; [Law]; debt $1000, damages $5000

plaintiff; 1869 July; pg 130; GD 148; Law; debt $1000, damages $5000

Morrison, James

defendant; 1871 Jan; pg 191; GD 207; Law; trespass damages $2000

Morrison, Sidney B

plaintiff; 1869 Jan; pg 109; GD 118; [Law]; debt $1000, damages $5000

plaintiff; 1869 July; pg 130; GD 148; Law; debt $1000, damages $5000

plaintiff; 1870 Jan; pg 147; GD 148; Law; debt $1000, damages $5000

Morrow, Thomas

plaintiff; 1868 July; pg 84; GD 69; Law; mechanic lien

plaintiff; 1868 Mar; pg 69; GD 69; Law; mechanic lien

plaintiff; 1869 July; pg 120; GD 69; Law; mechanics lien

Mosher, Calvin J

plaintiff; 1872 Jan; pg 267; GD 283; Chancery; divorce

Mosher, Ellen

defendant; 1872 Jan; pg 267; GD 283; Chancery; divorce

N

Neikirk, Henry

plaintiff; 1868 July; pg 92; GD 95; Law; trespass

plaintiff; 1868 Mar; pg 75; GD 81; Law; trespass

plaintiff; 1868 Mar; pg 75; GD 82; Law; effectment

plaintiff; 1868 Mar; pg 88; GD 81; Law; trespass

plaintiff; 1869 Jan; pg 106; GD 81; [Law]; trespass, $1000 damages

Niwot Mining Company, cont.
  defendant; 1871 Jan; pg 178; GD
    126; Law; mechanics lien
  defendant; 1871 Jan; pg 179; GD
    128; Law; mechanics lien
  defendant; 1871 Jan; pg 181; GD
    152; Law; mechanics lien
  defendant; 1871 Jan; pg 181; GD
    150; Law; mechanics lien
  defendant; 1871 June; pg 218; GD
    126; Law; mechanics lien
  defendant; 1871 June; pg 218; GD
    128; Law; mechanics lien
  defendant; 1871 June; pg 219; GD
    150; Law; mechanics lien
  defendant; 1871 June; pg 219; GD
    126; Law; mechanics lien
  defendant; 1871 June; pg 220; GD
    152; Law; mechanics lien
  defendant; 1872 Jan; pg 246; GD
    125; Law; mechanics lien
  defendant; 1872 Jan; pg 246; GD
    150; Law; mechanics lien
  defendant; 1872 Jan; pg 247; GD
    128; Law; mechanics lien
  defendant; 1872 Jan; pg 247; GD
    126; Law; mechanics lien
  defendant; 1872 Jan; pg 248; GD
    152; Law; mechanics lien

Noblet [Noblit], Samuel
  plaintiff; 1871 Jan; pg 180; GD
    145; Law

Noblet [Noblit], Samuel L
  defendant; 1867 Mar; pg 2; Crimi-
    nal; indictment for larceny
  plaintiff; 1869 July; pg 128; GD
    145; Law; appeal
  plaintiff; 1870 Jan; pg 146; GD
    145; Law; appeal

Noblit, Samuel T
  plaintiff; [1872 Jan]; pg 319; GD
    145; Law; appeal

O

Orchard, John
  plaintiff; 1872 Jan; pg 261; GD 300;
    Law; assumpsit, damages $6000
  defendant; 1872 Jan; pg 262; GD
    302; Law; mechanics lien

Orchard, Thomas
  plaintiff; 1872 Jan; pg 261; GD 300;
    Law; assumpsit, damages $6000
  defendant; 1872 Jan; pg 262; GD
    302; Law; mechanics lien

Orvis, Harrison F
  defendant; 1871 June; pg 211; GD
    244; Criminal; indictment for
    setting timber on fire
  defendant; 1872 Jan; pg 240; GD
    244; Criminal; indictment for
    setting timber on fire

Osborn, Daniel O
  defendant; 1870 Jan; pg 160; GD
    182; Law; assumpsit

Osborn, William H
  defendant; 1870 Jan; pg 160; GD
    182; Law; assumpsit

Owens, Hugh
  defendant; 1869 Jan; pg 104; GD
    117; Criminal; assault & battery,
    appealed from Justice

Oyler, Thomas
  plaintiff; 1868 Mar; pg 75; GD 81;
    Law; trespass

Parlin, David, cont.

plaintiff; 1867 Mar; pg 5; Law; appeal

defendant; 1868 July; pg 92; GD 95; Law; trespass

defendant; 1868 July; pg 94; GD 99; Law; trespass

defendant; 1868 July; pg 94; GD 98; Law; trespass

defendant; 1868 July; pg 95; GD 100; Law; trespass

defendant; 1868 July; pg 95; GD 101; Law; trespass

defendant; 1868 July; pg 96; GD 102; Law; trespass

defendant; 1868 July; pg 96; GD 103; Law; [trespass]

defendant; 1868 July; pg 97; GD 104; Law; trespass

defendant; 1868 Mar; pg 87; GD 79; Law; trespass

defendant; 1868 Mar; pg 87; GD 78; Law; trespass

defendant; 1868 Mar; pg 88; GD 80; Law; trespass

defendant; 1869 Jan; pg 105; GD 78; [Law]; trespass, $5000 damages

defendant; 1869 Jan; pg 108; GD 98; [Law]; trespass, $5000 damages

defendant; 1869 July; pg 117; GD 78; Law; trespass, $5000 damages

defendant; 1869 July; pg 118; GD 99; Law; trespass, $5000 damages

Parlin, Matilda

plaintiff; 1872 Jan; pg 257; GD 292; Law; trespass, damage $5000

defendant; 1872 Jan; pg 270; GD 306; Chancery; application to appoint appraisers

Partridge & Morrison

plaintiff; 1869 Jan; pg 109; GD 118; [Law]; debt $1000, damages $5000

plaintiff; 1869 July; pg 130; GD 148; Law; debt $1000, damages $5000

Partridge, James W

plaintiff; 1869 Jan; pg 109; GD 118; [Law]; debt $1000, damages $5000

plaintiff; 1869 July; pg 130; GD 148; Law; debt $1000, damages $5000

plaintiff; 1870 Jan; pg 147; GD 148; Law; debt $1000, damages $5000

Partridge, Lucy

plaintiff; 1868 July; pg 89; GD 89; Law; replevin

Patter, Warren

defendant; 1867 Nov; pg 57; Criminal; indictment for larceny

Peabody, Daniel G

plaintiff; 1872 Jan; pg 256; GD 288; Law; assumpsit, damages $1500

Pease, Abbie F

plaintiff; 1868 July; pg 99; GD 106; Law [Chancery]; divorce

People of Colorado Territory, cont.

plaintiff; 1868 Mar; pg 59; GD 1; Criminal; indictment for assault with intent to kill

plaintiff; 1868 Mar; pg 59; GD 2; Criminal; indictment for murder

plaintiff; 1868 Mar; pg 60; GD 45; Criminal; indictment for larceny

plaintiff; 1868 Mar; pg 60; GD 41; Criminal; assault with intent to inflict bodily injury

plaintiff; 1868 Mar; pg 61; GD 67; Criminal; information for gambling

plaintiff; 1868 Mar; pg 78; GD 86; Criminal; indictment for obstructing public hyway

plaintiff; 1868 Mar; pg 78; GD 85; Criminal; indictment for larceny

plaintiff; 1868 Mar; pg 78; GD 84; Criminal; indictment for resisting officer

plaintiff; 1869 Jan; pg 102; GD 67; Criminal; indictment for obstructing high way

plaintiff; 1869 Jan; pg 102; GD 67; Criminal; information for gambling

plaintiff; 1869 Jan; pg 103; GD 108; Criminal; indictment for larceny

plaintiff; 1869 Jan; pg 103; GD 110; Criminal; indictment for murder

plaintiff; 1869 Jan; pg 104; GD 123; Criminal; larceny

plaintiff; 1869 Jan; pg 104; GD 117; Criminal; assault & battery, appealed from Justice

plaintiff; 1869 Jan; pg 109; GD 118; [Law]; debt $1000, damages $5000

plaintiff; 1869 July; pg 115; GD 123; Criminal; larceny

plaintiff; 1869 July; pg 115; GD 67; Criminal; information for gambling

plaintiff; 1869 July; pg 116; GD 110; Criminal; murder

plaintiff; 1869 July; pg 116; GD 108; Criminal; larceny

plaintiff; 1869 July; pg 116; GD 110; Criminal; recognizance

plaintiff; 1869 July; pg 125; GD 137; Law; action debt $1000, damages $1000

plaintiff; 1869 July; pg 130; GD 148; Law; debt $1000, damages $5000

plaintiff; 1869 July; pg 138; GD 115; Criminal; indictment for larceny

plaintiff; 1870 [1871] Jan; pg 172; GD 190; Criminal; indictment for keeping open a tippling house on the Sabbath day

plaintiff; 1870 [1871] Jan; pg 172; GD 191; Criminal; indictment for selling liquor without a license

plaintiff; 1870 Jan; pg 139; GD 108; Criminal; indictment for malicious mischief

plaintiff; 1870 Jan; pg 139; GD 67; Criminal; information for gambling

plaintiff; 1870 Jan; pg 140; Criminal; selling liquor without license

People of Colorado Territory, cont.

plaintiff; 1871 Jan; pg 175; GD 197; Criminal; indictment for keeping a building and room to be used for gambling

plaintiff; 1871 Jan; pg 176; Criminal

plaintiff; 1871 Jan; pg 176; GD 235; Criminal

plaintiff; 1871 Jan; pg 176; GD 229; Criminal; to keep the peace

plaintiff; 1871 Jan; pg 176; GD 208; Criminal; indictment for perjury from Jefferson County

plaintiff; 1871 Jan; pg 177; GD 237; Criminal; assault &c

plaintiff; 1871 Jan; pg 177; GD 236; Criminal; indict larceny

plaintiff; 1871 Jan; pg 179; GD 137; Law; motion of debt $1000, damages $1000

plaintiff; 1871 June; pg 206; GD 110; Criminal; indictment for murder

plaintiff; 1871 June; pg 206; GD 189; Criminal; indictment for keeping open gambling house

plaintiff; 1871 June; pg 207; GD 190; Criminal; indictment for keeping open gambling house on the Sabbath day

plaintiff; 1871 June; pg 207; GD 191; Criminal; indictment for selling liquor without a license

plaintiff; 1871 June; pg 208; GD 229; Criminal; Keep the Peace

plaintiff; 1871 June; pg 208; GD 188; Criminal; indictment for keeping open gambling house & exhibiting gambling devices

plaintiff; 1871 June; pg 209; GD 240; Criminal; indictment for keeping open a tippling house on the Sabbath day

plaintiff; 1871 June; pg 209; GD 241; Criminal; indictment for keeping open a tippling house on the Sabbath day

plaintiff; 1871 June; pg 210; GD 242; Criminal; indictment for keeping a gambling house

plaintiff; 1871 June; pg 210; GD 243; Criminal; indictment for keeping a gambling house

plaintiff; 1871 June; pg 211; GD 244; Criminal; indictment for setting timber on fire

plaintiff; 1871 June; pg 211; GD 245; Criminal; indictment for setting timber on fire

plaintiff; 1871 June; pg 212; GD 247; Criminal; indictment for keeping tippling house open on the Sabbath day

plaintiff; 1871 June; pg 212; GD 246; Criminal; indictment for keeping tippling house open on the Sabbath day

plaintiff; 1871 June; pg 213; GD 249; Criminal; indictment for larceny

plaintiff; 1871 June; pg 213; GD 248; Criminal; indictment for keeping tippling house open on the Sabbath day

plaintiff; 1871 June; pg 214; GD 237; Criminal; indictment for assault with intent to kill

Perdue, Alison
defendant; 1872 Jan; pg 269; GD 295; Chancery; divorce

Perdue, Anna
plaintiff; 1872 Jan; pg 269; GD 295; Chancery; divorce

Perkins & Cook
attorney for plaintiff; 1867 Nov; pg 56; GD 64; Chancery; injunction
attorney for plaintiff; 1868 Mar; pg 63; GD 30; Law; trespass

Perkins, Charles E
defendant; 1872 Jan; pg 262; GD 302; Law; mechanics lien

Perkins, G W
attorney for plaintiff; 1871 Jan; pg 203; GD 224; Chancery

Perkins, Theodore E
defendant; 1872 Jan; pg 261; GD 300; Law; assumpsit, damages $6000

Phillips, Stephen
defendant; 1867 Nov; pg 48; GD 48; Law; trespass
defendant; 1867 Nov; pg 56; GD 64; Chancery; injunction
defendant; 1868 Mar; pg 65; GD 48; Law; trespass

Polly, W D
defendant; 1871 Jan; pg 197; GD 227; Law; debt, $600
defendant; 1871 June; pg 221; GD 227; Law; debt $600, damages $600
defendant; 1872 Jan; pg 254; GD 227; Law; debt, $600, damage $600

Pomeroy & Henry
defendant; 1872 Jan; pg 259; GD 296; Law; assumpsit, debt $2000

Pomeroy, James V
plaintiff; 1870 Jan; pg 149; GD 160; Law; replevin
defendant; 1872 Jan; pg 259; GD 296; Law; assumpsit, debt $2000

Post
attorney for defendant; 1867 Nov; pg 54; GD 60; Law; mechanic lien
attorney for plaintiff; 1867 Nov; pg 56; GD 64; Chancery; injunction
attorney for defendant; 1868 July; pg 84; GD 60; Law; mechanic lien
attorney for defendant; 1868 Mar; pg 64; GD 46; Law; mechanic lien
attorney for plaintiff; 1868 Mar; pg 73; GD 78; Law; trespass
attorney for plaintiff; 1869 Jan; pg 105; GD 78; [Law]; trespass, $5000 damages
attorney for defendant; 1869 Jan; pg 105; GD 46; [Law]; mechanics lien
attorney for defendant; 1869 Jan; pg 111; GD 60; [Law]; mechanics lien
attorney for plaintiff; 1869 July; pg 115; GD 67; Criminal; information for gambling
attorney for plaintiff; 1869 July; pg 116; GD 110; Criminal; murder
attorney for defendant; 1869 July; pg 117; GD 46; Law; mechanics lien

Post, C C

attorney for plaintiff; 1870 Jan; pg 141; GD 110; Criminal; indictment for murder

attorney for plaintiff; 1870 Jan; pg 142; GD 156; Criminal; indictment for selling liquor without license

attorney for plaintiff; 1870 Jan; pg 165; GD 187; Criminal; indictment for keeping tippling house open on the Sabbath day

attorney for plaintiff; 1870 Jan; pg 165; GD 186; Criminal; indictment for selling liquor without license

attorney for plaintiff; 1870 Jan; pg 166; GD 188; Criminal; indictment for keeping a house for gambling and for keeping and exhibiting gambling devices

Pound, Bryan

defendant; 1869 July; pg 136; GD 134; Chancery

Pound, Byron

defendant; 1870 Jan; pg 164; GD 134; Chancery; chancery

defendant; 1871 Jan; pg 204; GD 134; Chancery

Pound, Charlie

defendant; 1869 July; pg 136; GD 134; Chancery

defendant; 1870 Jan; pg 164; GD 134; Chancery; chancery

Pound, Charline

defendant; 1871 Jan; pg 204; GD 134; Chancery

Pound, D

plaintiff; 1868 July; pg 90; GD 90; Law; covenant

Pound, Daniel

defendant; 1869 July; pg 136; GD 134; Chancery

deceased; 1871 Jan; pg 204; GD 134; Chancery

Pound, Elias

defendant; 1869 July; pg 136; GD 134; Chancery

Pound, Elias S

defendant; 1870 Jan; pg 164; GD 134; Chancery; chancery

defendant; 1871 Jan; pg 204; GD 134; Chancery

Pound, Ephraim

defendant; 1869 July; pg 136; GD 134; Chancery

defendant; 1870 Jan; pg 164; GD 134; Chancery; chancery

defendant; 1871 Jan; pg 204; GD 134; Chancery

defendant; 1872 Jan; pg 258; GD 293; Law; action of debt, $10,000, damages $3,500

Pound, Immagene

defendant; 1869 July; pg 136; GD 134; Chancery

defendant; 1870 Jan; pg 164; GD 134; Chancery; chancery

Pound, Imogene

defendant; 1871 Jan; pg 204; GD 134; Chancery

Pound, Isabella

defendant; 1870 Jan; pg 164; GD 134; Chancery; chancery

Pound, Isabella B
defendant; 1871 Jan; pg 204; GD
134; Chancery
defendant; 1869 July; pg 136; GD
134; Chancery

Pound, Joseph
defendant; 1869 July; pg 136; GD
134; Chancery
defendant; 1870 Jan; pg 164; GD
134; Chancery; chancery
defendant; 1871 Jan; pg 204; GD
134; Chancery

Pound, Matilda S M
defendant; 1869 July; pg 136; GD
134; Chancery
defendant; 1870 Jan; pg 164; GD
134; Chancery; chancery
defendant; 1871 Jan; pg 204; GD
134; Chancery

Pound, Millie
defendant; 1870 Jan; pg 164; GD
134; Chancery; chancery
defendant; 1871 Jan; pg 204; GD
134; Chancery

Pound, William
plaintiff; 1868 July; pg 90; GD 90;
Law; covenant
plaintiff; 1869 July; pg 124; GD
132; Law; attachment
defendant; 1870 Jan; pg 164; GD
134; Chancery; chancery

Pound, Willie
defendant; 1869 July; pg 136; GD
134; Chancery

Pound, Wm
defendant; 1869 July; pg 136; GD
134; Chancery

Powell, Peter
plaintiff; 1869 July; pg 124; GD
136; Law; attachment

Pratt, Stafford J
plaintiff; 1870 Jan; pg 151; GD
164; Law; attachment

Putman (Berkley, Brown & Putman)
attorney for plaintiff; 1872 Jan; pg
246; GD 125; Law; mechanics
lien
attorney for plaintiff; 1872 Jan; pg
246; GD 150; Law; mechanics
lien
attorney for defendant; 1872 Jan;
pg 247; GD 128; Law; mechanics lien
attorney for defendant; 1872 Jan;
pg 251; GD 266; Law; unlawful
forcible entry & detainer
attorney for defendant; 1872 Jan;
pg 251; GD 263; Law; trespass,
damages $2000
attorney for plaintiff; 1872 Jan; pg
263; GD 212; Chancery; bill for
exceeding their authority and
other illegal proceedings
attorney for defendant; 1872 Jan;
pg 265; GD 291; Chancery; writ
of injunction

Putman (Brown & Putman)
attorney for plaintiff; 1871 June; pg
226; GD 261; Law; attachment
attorney for plaintiff; 1872 Jan; pg
248; GD 261; Law; attachment
attorney for defendant; 1872 Jan;
pg 249; GD 269; Law; appeal

Putman (Brown & Putman), cont.

attorney for plaintiff; 1872 Jan; pg 250; GD 250; Law; debt $3000, damages $3000

Putman (Brown, Harrison & Putman)

attorney for plaintiff; 1871 Jan; pg 192; GD 214; Law; debt, damages $300

attorney for plaintiff; 1871 Jan; pg 193; GD 216; Law; plea of debt, damages $700

R

Rackwell

attorney for plaintiff; 1870 Jan; pg 148; GD 152; Law; mechanics lien

Ramage, William W

plaintiff; 1872 Jan; pg 261; GD 300; Law; assumpsit, damages $6000

defendant; 1872 Jan; pg 262; GD 302; Law; mechanics lien

Rannells (S F Rannells & Son)

defendant; 1872 Jan; pg 259; GD 297; Law; assumpsit, damage $1000

Rannells, Benjamin B

defendant; 1872 Jan; pg 259; GD 297; Law; assumpsit, damage $1000

Rannells, Samuel F

defendant; 1872 Jan; pg 259; GD 297; Law; assumpsit, damage $1000

Rannells, William N

defendant; 1872 Jan; pg 259; GD 297; Law; assumpsit, damage $1000

Raynor, Arthur G

defendant; 1868 July; pg 98; GD 68; Chancery; foreclosure of mortgage

defendant; 1868 Mar; pg 77; GD 68; Chancery; foreclosure of mortgage

defendant; 1869 Jan; pg 112; GD 68; Chancery; foreclosure of mortgage

Reed

attorney for plaintiff; 1871 Jan; pg 195; GD 220; Law; appeal

Reed, C

District Attorney; 1871 Jan; pg 176; GD 208; Criminal; indictment for perjury from Jefferson County

attorney for plaintiff; 1871 June; pg 215; GD 270; Criminal; to keep the peace

attorney for plaintiff; 1871 June; pg 216; GD 271; Criminal; to keep the peace

attorney for plaintiff; 1871 June; pg 229; GD 272; Law; assumpsit, damages $1000

attorney for plaintiff; 1872 Jan; pg 253; GD 272; Law; assumpsit, damages $1000

attorney for plaintiff; 1872 Jan; pg 258; GD 293; Law; action of debt, $10,000, damages $3,500

attorney for plaintiff; 1872 Jan; pg
260; GD 299; Law; assumpsit,
damage, $1200

Reed, Clint
attorney for plaintiff; 1872 Jan; pg
261; GD 300; Law; assumpsit,
damages $6000

Reed, Clinton
District Attorney; 1870 [1871]
Jan; pg 172; GD 190; Criminal;
indictment for keeping open a
tippling house on the Sabbath
day
District Attorney; 1870 [1871]
Jan; pg 172; GD 191; Criminal;
indictment for selling liquor
without a license
attorney for plaintiff; 1871 Jan; pg
171; GD 110; Criminal; indictment for murder
District Attorney; 1871 Jan; pg
173; GD 188; Criminal; indictment for keeping a house for
gambling and for keeping and
exhibiting gambling devices
District Attorney; 1871 Jan; pg
173; GD 194; Criminal; indictment for keeping open a tippling
house on the Sabbath day
District Attorney; 1871 Jan; pg
175; GD 197; Criminal; indictment for keeping a building and
room to be used for gambling
attorney for plaintiff; 1871 Jan; pg
198; GD 232; Law; assumpsit
attorney for plaintiff; 1871 Jan; pg
198; GD 231; Law; attachment

Reichart [Richart], Henry
defendant; 1867 Nov; pg 48; GD
47; Law; debt

Reynolds, Samuel F
defendant; 1869 Jan; pg 109; GD
119; [Law]; assumpsit

Rhodes, E M
plaintiff; 1867 Mar; pg 26; Law;
appeal

Rice, William H
defendant; 1872 Jan; pg 258; GD
294; Law; appeal

Richardson, Charles S
defendant; 1872 Jan; pg 261; GD
300; Law; assumpsit, damages
$6000
defendant; 1872 Jan; pg 262; GD
302; Law; mechanics lien

Richardson, Isaac
defendant; 1867 Mar; pg 12; Law;
appeal

Richardson, Isac [Isaac]
defendant; 1871 June; pg 225; GD
259; Law; assumpsit, damages
$2000

Richardson, John
defendant; 1868 July; pg 84; GD
69; Law; mechanic lien

Richardson, Stowe & Company
defendant; 1872 Jan; pg 261; GD
300; Law; assumpsit, damages
$6000
defendant; 1872 Jan; pg 262; GD
302; Law; mechanics lien

Richart, Henry
defendant; 1867 Mar; pg 7; Law; replevin
defendant; 1867 Nov; pg 54; GD 9; Law; replevin, at issue
defendant; 1868 Mar; pg 65; GD 47; Law; debt

Richman, Thomas J
plaintiff; 1871 Jan; pg 198; GD 231; Law; attachment

Rink, Francis
plaintiff; 1867 Nov; pg 51; GD 54; Law; mechanic lien
plaintiff; 1868 July; pg 83; GD 54; Law; mechanic lien
plaintiff; 1868 Mar; pg 67; GD 54; Law; mechanic lien

Ritchie, John W
defendant; 1871 June; pg 236; GD 265; Chancery; bill for foreclosure
defendant; 1872 Jan; pg 264; GD 265; Chancery; bill for foreclosure of mortgage

Roberts, Sealy [Selah] F
defendant; 1867 Mar; pg 3; Law; trespass

Robertson
[Special] Master; 1869 Jan; pg 113; GD 121; Chancery; divorce

Robinson
[Special] Master; 1869 Jan; pg 114; GD 115; [Chancery]; foreclosure of mortgage

Robinson, Daniel A
[Special] Master; 1869 July; pg 136; GD 135; Chancery; foreclosure of mortgage

Special] Master; 1869 July; pg 137; GD 140; Chancery; divorce

Rocky Mountain National Bank
plaintiff; 1871 Jan; pg 198; GD 228; Law; attachment

Roose, Thomas
plaintiff; 1870 Jan; pg 148; GD 152; Law; mechanics lien

Rothrick [Rothrock], John
defendant; 1871 Jan; pg 174; GD 199; Criminal; indictment for selling liquor without a license
defendant; 1871 Jan; pg 174; GD 196; Criminal; indictment for keeping open a tippling house on the Sabbath day

Russell, Henry M
defendant; [1868 July]; pg 93; GD 96; Law; trespass
defendant; [1868 July]; pg 93; GD 97; Law; trespass
defendant; 1868 July; pg 92; GD 95; Law; trespass
defendant; 1868 July; pg 94; GD 99; Law; trespass
defendant; 1868 July; pg 94; GD 98; Law; trespass
defendant; 1868 July; pg 95; GD 101; Law; trespass
defendant; 1868 July; pg 95; GD 100; Law; trespass
defendant; 1868 July; pg 96; GD 103; Law; [trespass]
defendant; 1868 July; pg 96; GD 102; Law; trespass
defendant; 1868 July; pg 97; GD 104; Law; trespass
defendant; 1868 Mar; pg 87; GD 79; Law; trespass

defendant; 1868 Mar; pg 87; GD
78; Law; trespass

defendant; 1868 Mar; pg 88; GD
80; Law; trespass

defendant; 1869 Jan; pg 105; GD
78; [Law]; trespass, $5000 dam-
ages

defendant; 1869 Jan; pg 108; GD
98; [Law]; trespass, $5000 dam-
ages

defendant; 1869 July; pg 117; GD
78; Law; trespass, $5000 dam-
ages

defendant; 1869 July; pg 118; GD
99; Law; trespass, $5000 dam-
ages

S

S F Rannalls & Son

defendant; 1872 Jan; pg 259; GD
297; Law; assumpsit, damage
$1000

Safely, Alexander

defendant; 1871 Jan; pg 191; GD
213; Law; trespass damages
$1000

Safely, James

defendant; 1871 Jan; pg 198; GD
230; Law

Sanford, Francis A

plaintiff; 1871 June; pg 225; GD
258; Law; assumpsit, damages
$2000

Savits, James B

defendant; 1869 Jan; pg 104; GD
123; Criminal; larceny

defendant; 1869 July; pg 115; GD
123; Criminal; larceny

Sayre

attorney for plaintiff; 1868 July; pg
91; GD 93; Law; trespass

attorney for plaintiff; 1868 July; pg
92; GD 94; Law; trespass

attorney for plaintiff; 1869 Jan; pg
107; GD 94; [Law]; assumpsit

attorney for plaintiff; 1869 Jan; pg
114; GD 115; [Chancery]; foreclosure of mortgage

attorney for plaintiff; 1869 July; pg
132; GD 153; Law; assumpsit

attorney for plaintiff; 1869 July; pg
136; GD 135; Chancery; foreclosure of mortgage

Sayre & others

attorney for plaintiff; 1868 July; pg
92; GD 95; Law; trespass

Sayre, Daniel

plaintiff; 1869 Jan; pg 114; GD
115; [Chancery]; foreclosure of
mortgage

plaintiff; 1869 July; pg 137; GD
115; Chancery; foreclosure of
mortgage

Sayre, Post & Morgan

attorney for plaintiff; [1868 July];
pg 93; GD 96; Law; trespass

attorney for plaintiff; [1868 July];
pg 93; GD 97; Law; trespass

attorney for plaintiff; 1868 July; pg
94; GD 99; Law; trespass

attorney for plaintiff; 1868 July; pg
94; GD 98; Law; trespass

attorney for plaintiff; 1868 July; pg
95; GD 101; Law; trespass

Sayre, Post & Morgan
attorney for plaintiff; 1868 July; pg 95; GD 100; Law; trespass
attorney for plaintiff; 1868 July; pg 96; GD 103; Law; [trespass]
attorney for plaintiff; 1868 July; pg 96; GD 102; Law; trespass
attorney for plaintiff; 1868 July; pg 97; GD 104; Law; trespass
attorney for plaintiff; 1868 Mar; pg 87; GD 79; Law; trespass
attorney for plaintiff; 1868 Mar; pg 88; GD 80; Law; trespass

Scott, J D
defendant; 1869 Jan; pg 109; GD 119; [Law]; assumpsit

Scott, Thomas
defendant; 1870 Jan; pg 162; GD 158; Chancery
defendant; 1871 Jan; pg 199; GD 158; Chancery
plaintiff; 1871 June; pg 217; GD 250; Law; debt $3000, damages $3000
defendant; 1871 June; pg 233; GD 158; Chancery; injunction
plaintiff; 1872 Jan; pg 250; GD 250; Law; debt $3000, damages $3000
defendant; 1872 Jan; pg 263; GD 158; Chancery; injunction

Scouten, D G
plaintiff; 1871 June; pg 230; GD 275; Law; assumpsit

Seaman, Herman
defendant; 1872 Jan; pg 249; GD 269; Law; appeal

Sears, Jasper
plaintiff; 1867 Nov; pg 48; GD 48; Law; trespass
plaintiff; 1867 Nov; pg 56; GD 64; Chancery; injunction
plaintiff; 1868 Mar; pg 65; GD 48; Law; trespass

Sears, William F
defendant; 1871 June; pg 209; GD 241; Criminal; indictment for keeping open a tippling house on the Sabbath day

Seman, Herman
defendant; 1871 June; pg 229; GD 269; Law; appeal

Shanahan, Patrick
defendant; 1867 Mar; pg 23; Law; trespass
defendant; 1867 Nov; pg 44; GD 30; Law; trespass at issue
defendant; 1868 Mar; pg 63; GD 30; Law; trespass

Sheldon, Joseph
defendant; 1871 June; pg 217; GD 254; Law

Shelton, Joseph M
plaintiff; 1869 July; pg 129; GD 146; Law; replevin

Sherman, Cilenda
defendant; 1868 July; pg 98; GD 105; Chancery; divorce

Sherman, Isaac
plaintiff; 1868 July; pg 98; GD 105; Chancery; divorce

Sherwood, Jesse M
plaintiff; 1867 Nov; pg 50; GD 52; Law; replevin

plaintiff; 1871 Jan; pg 192; GD
214; Law; debt, damages $300

Shores, Frank
defendant; 1869 July; pg 127; GD
142; Law; attachment

Shourds, John
plaintiff; [1868 July]; pg 93; GD 97;
Law; trespass

Simpson, James
defendant; 1868 July; pg 100; GD
108; Law [Criminal]; indictment
for larceny
defendant; 1869 Jan; pg 103; GD
108; Criminal; indictment for
larceny
defendant; 1869 July; pg 116; GD
108; Criminal; larceny
defendant; 1870 Jan; pg 139; GD
108; Criminal; indictment for
malicious mischief

Slack, Andrew J
plaintiff; 1868 July; pg 96; GD 103;
Law; [trespass]

Slater, Manerva Jane
plaintiff; 1871 June; pg 235; GD
260; Chancery; divorce

Slater, William C
defendant; 1871 June; pg 235; GD
260; Chancery; divorce

Smart, Charles W
plaintiff; 1870 Jan; pg 152; GD
167; Law; attachment

Smith
attorney for plaintiff; 1868 July; pg
97; GD 105; Law; assumpsit
attorney for defendant; 1869 July;
pg 120; GD 29; Law; assumpsit

attorney for plaintiff; 1869 July; pg
133; GD 154; Law; assumpsit

Smith & Beckwith
defendant; 1871 June; pg 225; GD
258; Law; assumpsit, damages
$2000

Smith, Austin
defendant; 1867 Nov; pg 54; Law;
appeal
plaintiff; 1869 July; pg 125; GD
138; Law; mechanics lien
plaintiff; 1870 Jan; pg 145; GD
138; Law; mechanics lien
plaintiff; 1871 Jan; pg 180; GD
138; Law; mechanics lien
defendant; 1871 Jan; pg 200; GD
210; Chancery; foreclosure of
mortgage

Smith, Francis M
defendant; 1869 July; pg 124; GD
132; Law; attachment

Smith, G
defendant; 1870 Jan; pg 147; GD
148; Law; debt $1000, damages
$5000

Smith, Harriet D
defendant; 1871 Jan; pg 201; GD
211; Chancery; foreclosure of
mortgage

Smith, James M
defendant; 1867 Nov; pg 50; GD
53; Law; Appeal
defendant; 1868 July; pg 82; GD
52; Law; appellant
defendant; 1868 Mar; pg 66; GD
52; Law; appellant
defendant; 1869 July; pg 124; GD
132; Law; attachment

Smith, James M, cont.
defendant; 1871 June; pg 225; GD 258; Law; assumpsit, damages $2000

Smith, John W
plaintiff; 1871 Jan; pg 200; GD 204; Chancery; foreclosure of mortgage
plaintiff; 1871 Jan; pg 200; GD 210; Chancery; foreclosure of mortgage
plaintiff; 1871 Jan; pg 201; GD 211; Chancery; foreclosure of mortgage

Smith, Jonathan S
defendant; 1872 Jan; pg 265; GD 291; Chancery; writ of injunction

Smith, Marinus G
defendant; 1869 Jan; pg 109; GD 118; [Law]; debt $1000, damages $5000
defendant; 1869 July; pg 130; GD 148; Law; debt $1000, damages $5000

Smith, William H
defendant; 1867 Nov; pg 57; Criminal; indictment for murder

Snider, C B
defendant; 1871 Jan; pg 187; GD 184; Law; mechanics lien
notice given; 1870 Jan; pg 161; GD 184; Law; mechanics lien
defendant; 1871 June; pg 223; GD 184; Law; mechanics lien

Snyder, Hanson
plaintiff; 1869 July; pg 123; GD 128; Law; mechanics lien

plaintiff; 1870 Jan; pg 144; GD 128; Law; mechanics lien
plaintiff; 1871 Jan; pg 179; GD 128; Law; mechanics lien
plaintiff; 1871 June; pg 218; GD 128; Law; mechanics lien
plaintiff; 1872 Jan; pg 247; GD 128; Law; mechanics lien
defendant; 1872 Jan; pg 265; GD 291; Chancery; writ of injunction

Solander, John
defendant; 1871 Jan; pg 175; Criminal

Solander, Mary
defendant; 1872 Jan; pg 245; GD 308; Criminal; indictment for manslaughter

Sommers, Wilhelm
defendant; 1869 Jan; pg 110; GD 120; [Law]; appeal

Sopris, Richard
plaintiff; 1867 Mar; pg 16; Law; appeal from the county commissioners

Soule, Albert G
plaintiff; 1867 Mar; pg 21; Law; assumpsit

Spalti, Henry
defendant; 1869 July; pg 133; GD 154; Law; assumpsit

Springall, Joseph
defendant; 1867 Nov; pg 40; GD 45; Criminal; indictment for larceny
defendant; 1867 Nov; pg 51; GD 53; Law; attachment

Stowe (Richardson, Stowe & Company)

defendant; 1872 Jan; pg 261; GD 300; Law; assumpsit, damages $6000

defendant; 1872 Jan; pg 262; GD 302; Law; mechanics lien

Stowe, Milton

defendant; 1872 Jan; pg 262; GD 302; Law; mechanics lien

Stowe, William H

defendant; 1872 Jan; pg 261; GD 300; Law; assumpsit, damages $6000

Streaver, Loyd

defendant; 1868 July; pg 100; GD 109; Law [Criminal]; indictment for malicious mischief

Sullivan, Jacob M

defendant; 1868 Mar; pg 70; GD 71; Law; trespass

defendant; 1868 July; pg 85; GD 71; Law; trespass

defendant; 1871 Jan; pg 202; GD 212; Chancery; bill for exceeding their authority and other illegal proceedings

defendant; 1871 June; pg 232; GD 212; Chancery; bill for exceeding their authority and other illegal proceedings

defendant; 1872 Jan; pg 263; GD 212; Chancery; bill for exceeding their authority and other illegal proceedings

T

Taft, Anna W

plaintiff; 1869 July; pg 135; GD 131; Chancery; divorce

Taft, Benj A

defendant; 1869 July; pg 135; GD 131; Chancery; divorce

Teller

attorney for defendant; 1868 Mar; pg 75; GD 81; Law; trespass

attorney for defendant; 1868 Mar; pg 75; GD 82; Law; effectment

attorney for defendant; 1869 Jan; pg 105; GD 78; [Law]; trespass, $5000 damages

attorney for defendant; 1869 Jan; pg 106; GD 81; [Law]; trespass, $1000 damages

Teller & Browne

attorney for defendant; 1868 Mar; pg 88; GD 81; Law; trespass

Teller & Johnson

attorney for plaintiff; 1872 Jan; pg 252; GD 272; Law; assumpsit, damages $500

Teller & others

attorney for defendant; 1868 Mar; pg 87; GD 79; Law; trespass

attorney for defendant; 1868 Mar; pg 87; GD 78; Law; trespass

attorney for defendant; 1868 Mar; pg 88; GD 80; Law; trespass

attorney for defendant; 1869 July; pg 118; GD 99; Law; trespass, $5000 damages

attorney for defendant; 1869 July;
pg 118; GD 81; Law; trespass,
$10,000 damages

Teller (Johnson & Teller)
attorney for plaintiff; 1871 Jan; pg
188; GD 201; Law; attachment
attorney for plaintiff; 1871 Jan; pg
188; GD 200; Law; trespass on
the case of premesis, attachment
attorney for plaintiff; 1871 Jan; pg
189; GD 202; Law; attachment
attorney for defendant; 1871 Jan;
pg 197; GD 226; Law; assumpsit
attorney for defendant; 1871 Jan;
pg 198; GD 232; Law; assumpsit
attorney for defendant; 1871 Jan;
pg 198; GD 231; Law; attachment
attorney for plaintiff; 1871 Jan; pg
198; GD 228; Law; attachment
attorney for defendant; 1871 Jan;
pg 205; GD 234; Law; appeal,
change of venue from Gilpin
County

Teller, Willard
plaintiff; 1871 June; pg 230; GD
273; Law; assumpsit, damages
$500
plaintiff; 1872 Jan; pg 252; GD 272;
Law; assumpsit, damages $500

Terrill, Thomas
plaintiff; 1870 Jan; pg 148; GD
152; Law; mechanics lien
plaintiff; 1871 Jan; pg 181; GD
152; Law; mechanics lien

Terry, Charles
plaintiff; 1868 July; pg 86; GD 76;
Law; appellant

plaintiff; 1868 July; pg 86; GD 75;
Law; trespass
plaintiff; 1868 Mar; pg 72; GD 76;
Law; appellant
plaintiff; 1868 Mar; pg 72; GD 75;
Law; appellant

Terry, John
plaintiff; 1868 July; pg 86; GD 75;
Law; trespass
plaintiff; 1868 July; pg 86; GD 76;
Law; appellant
plaintiff; 1868 Mar; pg 72; GD 75;
Law; appellant

Terry, John H
plaintiff; 1869 Jan; pg 108; GD
112; [Law]; attachment
plaintiff; 1869 July; pg 119; GD
112; Law; attachment

Terry, John O
plaintiff; 1868 Mar; pg 72; GD 76;
Law; appellant

Thomas, Jerome
defendant; 1870 Jan; pg 151; GD
165; Law; attachment
defendant; 1870 Jan; pg 161; GD
184; Law; mechanics lien
defendant; 1871 Jan; pg 187; GD
184; Law; mechanics lien
defendant; 1871 Jan; pg 189; GD
203; Law; trespass on the case
of premesis, damages $8000,
attachment
defendant; 1871 June; pg 223; GD
184; Law; mechanics lien
defendant; 1872 Jan; pg 256; GD
289; Law; assumpsit, damages
$400

Thomas, Jerome, cont.
defendant; 1872 Jan; pg 257; GD 290; Law; assumpsit, damages $200

Thomas, John W
plaintiff; 1871 June; pg 229; GD 272; Law; assumpsit, damages $1000
plaintiff; 1872 Jan; pg 253; GD 272; Law; assumpsit, damages $1000

Thompson, John
defendant; 1871 June; pg 211; GD 245; Criminal; indictment for setting timber on fire
defendant; 1872 Jan; pg 241; GD 245; Criminal; indictment for setting timber on fire

Todd, Wm Y
defendant; 1869 Jan; pg 109; GD 119; [Law]; assumpsit

Tourtellot & Squires
defendant; 1867 Mar; pg 15; Law; assumpsit
plaintiff; 1870 Jan; pg 151; GD 165; Law; attachment
plaintiff; 1871 Jan; pg 188; GD 200; Law; trespass on the case of premesis, attachment
plaintiff; 1871 Jan; pg 188; GD 201; Law; attachment

Tourtellot, Jonathan A
plaintiff; 1870 Jan; pg 151; GD 165; Law; attachment
plaintiff; 1871 Jan; pg 188; GD 200; Law; trespass on the case of premesis, attachment
plaintiff; 1871 Jan; pg 188; GD 201; Law; attachment

Tourtellot, Maria
plaintiff; 1872 Jan; pg 259; GD 296; Law; assumpsit, debt $2000

Towner, Lucinda
plaintiff; 1871 June; pg 233; GD 158; Chancery; divorce
plaintiff; 1872 Jan; pg 267; GD 255; Chancery; divorce

Towner, Mansfield
defendant; 1872 Jan; pg 262; GD 301; Law; replevin

Towner, Ruben [Reuben]
defendant; 1871 June; pg 215; GD 270; Criminal; to keep the peace
defendant; 1871 June; pg 233; GD 158; Chancery; divorce
defendant; 1872 Jan; pg 242; GD 270; Criminal; bound over to keep the peace
plaintiff; 1872 Jan; pg 262; GD 301; Law; replevin
defendant; 1872 Jan; pg 267; GD 255; Chancery; divorce

Trevan, William
plaintiff; 1871 Jan; pg 181; GD 152; Law; mechanics lien

Trevan, Wm
plaintiff; 1870 Jan; pg 148; GD 152; Law; mechanics lien

Trowbridge (Wright & Trowbridge)
attorney for plaintiff; 1872 Jan; pg 251; GD 266; Law; unlawful forcible entry & detainer
attorney for plaintiff; 1872 Jan; pg 251; GD 263; Law; trespass, damages $2000

Virden, John, cont.

defendant; 1871 June; pg 232; GD 212; Chancery; bill for exceeding their authority and other illegal proceedings

defendant; 1872 Jan; pg 263; GD 212; Chancery; bill for exceeding their authority and other illegal proceedings

appraiser; 1872 Jan; pg 270; GD 306; Chancery; application to appoint appraisers

W

Wade, Noble

plaintiff; 1871 Jan; pg 197; GD 227; Law; debt, $600

plaintiff; 1871 June; pg 221; GD 227; Law; debt $600, damages $600

plaintiff; 1872 Jan; pg 254; GD 227; Law; debt, $600, damage $600

Waeneke, Adolf

defendant; 1869 Jan; pg 112; GD 111; Chancery; divorce

Waeneke, Anna

plaintiff; 1869 Jan; pg 112; GD 111; Chancery; divorce

Wain, Elizabeth

defendant; 1868 July; pg 90; GD 90; Law; covenant

Wain, William

defendant; 1868 July; pg 90; GD 90; Law; covenant

Walcott, Horace A

defendant; 1870 Jan; pg 159; GD 181; Law; trespass on the case upon premises, damages $1000

plaintiff; 1870 Jan; pg 160; GD 182; Law; assumpsit

Wallace, John J

defendant; 1868 Mar; pg 70; GD 72; Law; debt

Ward, Calvin W

plaintiff; 1867 Mar; pg 28; Law; assumpsit

defendant; 1867 Nov; pg 55; GD 13; Chancery; foreclosure of mortgage

Ware, John M

defendant; 1871 Jan; pg 193; GD 216; Law; plea of debt, damages $700

Warren Hussey & Co

plaintiff; 1869 July; pg 125; GD 137; Law; action debt $1000, damages $1000

plaintiff; 1870 Jan; pg 145; GD 137; Law; action debt $1000, damages $1000

plaintiff; 1871 Jan; pg 179; GD 137; Law; motion of debt $1000, damages $1000

plaintiff; 1871 June; pg 227; GD 137; Law; actions of debt, damages $1000

plaintiff; 1872 Jan; pg 253; GD 137; Law; action of debt, damages $100

Washburn, Hiram E

defendant; 1871 June; pg 215; GD 253; Criminal; assault & battery

Wealch [Welch], Charles C
defendant; 1871 Jan; pg 187; GD
184; Law; mechanics lien

Webster, G W
defendant; 1871 June; pg 232; GD
212; Chancery; bill for exceeding their authority and other
illegal proceedings
defendant; 1872 Jan; pg 263; GD
212; Chancery; bill for exceeding their authority and other
illegal proceedings

Webster, Geo W
appraiser; 1872 Jan; pg 270; GD
306; Chancery; application to
appoint appraisers

Webster, George W
defendant; 1871 Jan; pg 202; GD
212; Chancery; bill for exceeding their authority and other
illegal proceedings

Wedge, Hugh
defendant; 1869 Jan; pg 108; GD
112; [Law]; attachment
defendant; 1869 July; pg 119; GD
112; Law; attachment

Weese, Columbus
plaintiff; 1867 Mar; pg 6; Law;
appeal

Welch, Charles C
defendant; 1871 June; pg 223; GD
184; Law; mechanics lien

Wellman & Nichols
defendant; 1871 Jan; pg 202; GD
212; Chancery; bill for exceeding their authority and other
illegal proceedings

defendant; 1871 June; pg 232; GD
212; Chancery; bill for exceeding their authority and other
illegal proceedings

Wellman, Luther C
plaintiff; 1871 Jan; pg 189; GD
202; Law; attachment
defendant; 1871 Jan; pg 202; GD
212; Chancery; bill for exceeding their authority and other
illegal proceedings
defendant; 1871 June; pg 232; GD
212; Chancery; bill for exceeding their authority and other
illegal proceedings
defendant; 1872 Jan; pg 263; GD
212; Chancery; bill for exceeding their authority and other
illegal proceedings

Wellman, Sylvanus
plaintiff; 1871 Jan; pg 189; GD
202; Law; attachment

Wells
attorney for defendant; 1867 Nov;
pg 46; GD 38; Law; appeal
attorney for plaintiff; 1867 Nov; pg
50; GD 53; Law; Appeal
attorney for plaintiff; 1867 Nov; pg
53; GD 59; Law; attachment
attorney for plaintiff; 1868 July; pg
82; GD 52; Law; appellant
attorney for plaintiff; 1868 July; pg
86; GD 75; Law; appellant
attorney for plaintiff; 1868 July; pg
86; GD 76; Law; appellant
attorney for defendant; 1868 Mar;
pg 64; GD 38; Law; appellant
attorney for plaintiff; 1868 Mar; pg
66; GD 52; Law; appellant

Wells, cont.

attorney for plaintiff; 1868 Mar; pg 72; GD 75; Law; appellant

attorney for plaintiff; 1868 Mar; pg 72; GD 76; Law; appellant

attorney for plaintiff; 1868 Mar; pg 73; GD 78; Law; trespass

attorney for plaintiff; 1869 Jan; pg 111; GD 114; [Law]; appeal

attorney for defendant; 1869 July; pg 121; GD 124; Law; appeal

attorney for defendant; 1869 July; pg 122; GD 127; Law; appeal

attorney for plaintiff; 1869 July; pg 135; GD 131; Chancery; divorce

attorney for plaintiff; 1871 Jan; pg 190; GD 206; Law; appeal

Wells (Decker & Wells)

attorney for defendant; 1868 July; pg 85; GD 71; Law; trespass

attorney for defendant; 1868 Mar; pg 70; GD 71; Law; trespass

Wells (E T Wells & Brown)

attorney for plaintiff; 1871 Jan; pg 197; GD 226; Law; assumpsit

Wells, Henry O

plaintiff; 1870 Jan; pg 154; GD 171; Law; mechanics lien

plaintiff; 1870 Jan; pg 155; GD 172; Law; attachment

plaintiff; 1871 Jan; pg 183; GD 172; Law; attachment

plaintiff; 1871 Jan; pg 183; GD 171; Law; mechanics lien

plaintiff; 1871 June; pg 224; GD 171; Law; mechanics lien

Wells, J H

attorney for defendant; 1870 Jan; pg 141; GD 154; Criminal; indictment for larceny

attorney for defendant; 1870 Jan; pg 145; GD 137; Law; action debt $1000, damages $1000

attorney for defendant; 1870 Jan; pg 152; GD 166; Law; appeal

attorney for defendant; 1871 June; pg 215; GD 253; Criminal; assault & battery

attorney for plaintiff; 1872 Jan; pg 249; GD 218; Law; mechanics lien

attorney for defendant; 1872 Jan; pg 253; GD 137; Law; action of debt, damages $100

attorney for plaintiff; 1872 Jan; pg 264; GD 265; Chancery; bill for foreclosure of mortgage

Wells, Jno H

Special Master; 1869 July; pg 135; GD 131; Chancery; divorce

Wells, John

attorney for defendant; 1869 July; pg 125; GD 137; Law; action debt $1000, damages $1000

Wells, John H

attorney; 1867 Nov; pg 37; Criminal; indictment for murder

attorney; 1867 Nov; pg 37; Criminal; indictment for assault with intent to kill

County Attorney; 1867 Nov; pg 38; GD 40; Criminal; indictment for defacing brand

Wetherbee, John, cont.

defendant; 1870 Jan; pg 155; GD 173; Law; attachment

defendant; 1870 Jan; pg 155; GD 172; Law; attachment

defendant; 1870 Jan; pg 156; GD 174; Law; mechanics lien

defendant; 1870 Jan; pg 156; GD 175; Law; mechanics lien

defendant; 1870 Jan; pg 157; GD 176; Law; attachment

defendant; 1870 Jan; pg 157; GD 177; Law; mechanics lien

defendant; 1870 Jan; pg 158; GD 178; Law; attachment

defendant; 1870 Jan; pg 161; GD 184; Law; mechanics lien

defendant; 1871 Jan; pg 182; GD 169; Law; mechanics lien

defendant; 1871 Jan; pg 182; GD 170; Law; attachment

defendant; 1871 Jan; pg 183; GD 171; Law; mechanics lien

defendant; 1871 Jan; pg 183; GD 172; Law; attachment

defendant; 1871 Jan; pg 184; GD 173; Law; attachment

defendant; 1871 Jan; pg 184; GD 174; Law; mechanics lien

defendant; 1871 Jan; pg 185; GD 176; Law; attachment

defendant; 1871 Jan; pg 185; GD 175; Law; mechanics lien

defendant; 1871 Jan; pg 186; GD 178; Law; attachment

defendant; 1871 Jan; pg 186; GD 177; Law; mechanics lien

defendant; 1871 Jan; pg 187; GD 184; Law; mechanics lien

defendant; 1871 Jan; pg 188; GD 201; Law; attachment

defendant; 1871 Jan; pg 188; GD 200; Law; trespass on the case of premesis, attachment

plaintiff; 1871 Jan; pg 189; GD 202; Law; attachment

defendant; 1871 Jan; pg 189; GD 203; Law; trespass on the case of premesis, damages $8000, attachment

defendant; 1871 June; pg 222; GD 175; Law; mechanics lien

defendant; 1871 June; pg 222; GD 177; Law; mechanics lien

defendant; 1871 June; pg 223; GD 169; Law; mechanics lien

defendant; 1871 June; pg 223; GD 184; Law; mechanics lien

defendant; 1871 June; pg 224; GD 171; Law; mechanics lien

defendant; 1871 June; pg 224; GD 174; Law; mechanics lien

Wharton, Junius E

defendant; 1869 July; pg 128; GD 144; Law; mechanics lien

defendant; 1870 Jan; pg 149; GD 160; Law; replevin

defendant; 1870 Jan; pg 152; GD 167; Law; attachment

Whipple, Elizabeth A

defendant; 1871 June; pg 234; GD 257; Chancery; divorce

Whipple, Jeremiah W

plaintiff; 1867 Nov; pg 54; Law; appeal

plaintiff; 1871 June; pg 234; GD 257; Chancery; divorce

Wickham, Benj F, cont.
defendant; 1869 July; pg 118; GD
99; Law; trespass, $5000 damages

Wickham, Benjamin
defendant; 1868 Mar; pg 87; GD
78; Law; trespass

Wickham, Benjamin F
defendant; [1868 July]; pg 93; GD
97; Law; trespass
defendant; 1868 July; pg 95; GD
101; Law; trespass
defendant; 1868 July; pg 96; GD
103; Law; [trespass]
defendant; 1868 Mar; pg 87; GD
79; Law; trespass
defendant; 1868 Mar; pg 88; GD
80; Law; trespass

Widener [Widner], Amos
plaintiff; 1867 Mar; pg 27; Law;
assumpsit
plaintiff; 1867 Nov; pg 45; GD 36;
Law; assumpsit
plaintiff; 1868 Mar; pg 63; GD 36;
Law; assumpsit

Widner, Amos
plaintiff; 1868 July; pg 82; GD 36;
Law; assumpsit
defendant; 1870 Jan; pg 159; GD
180; Law; appeal
defendant; 1872 Jan; pg 262; GD
301; Law; appeal

Williams, John
defendant; 1872 Jan; pg 244; GD
304; Criminal; bound over to
keep the peace

Williams, Joseph
plaintiff; 1869 July; pg 121; GD
124; Law; appeal

Williams, Joseph B
plaintiff; 1870 Jan; pg 152; GD
166; Law; appeal

Wills, Samuel
plaintiff; 1870 Jan; pg 158; GD
179; Law; replevin

Wilson, Alonzo
defendant; 1869 July; pg 123; GD
130; Law; assumpsit

Wilson, John
defendant; 1871 Jan; pg 176; GD
235; Criminal
defendant; 1871 Jan; pg 177; GD
236; Criminal; indict larceny

Witter, Daniel
plaintiff; 1872 Jan; pg 266; GD 285;
Chancery; bill for foreclosure of
mortgage

Wolcott, Horace A
defendant; 1871 Jan; pg 187; GD
181; Law; trespass on the case
upon premises, damages $1000

Wolf, Joseph
defendant; [1868 July]; pg 93; GD
97; Law; trespass
defendant; [1868 July]; pg 93; GD
96; Law; trespass
defendant; 1868 July; pg 92; GD
95; Law; trespass
defendant; 1868 July; pg 94; GD
99; Law; trespass
defendant; 1868 July; pg 94; GD
98; Law; trespass

Wright, cont.

attorney for defendant; 1869 Jan; pg 105; GD 78; [Law]; trespass, $5000 damages

attorney for defendant; 1869 Jan; pg 106; GD 81; [Law]; trespass, $1000 damages

attorney for defendant; 1869 Jan; pg 107; GD 92; [Law]; assumpsit

attorney for plaintiff; 1869 Jan; pg 110; GD 120; [Law]; appeal

attorney for plaintiff; 1869 Jan; pg 111; GD 60; [Law]; mechanics lien

attorney for plaintiff; 1869 Jan; pg 114; GD 116; [Chancery]; divorce

attorney for plaintiff; 1869 July; pg 117; GD 46; Law; mechanics lien

attorney for plaintiff; 1869 July; pg 119; GD 60; Law; mechanics lien

attorney for plaintiff; 1869 July; pg 120; GD 69; Law; mechanics lien

attorney for plaintiff; 1869 July; pg 128; GD 145; Law; appeal

attorney for plaintiff; 1869 July; pg 129; GD 146; Law; replevin

attorney for plaintiff; 1869 July; pg 134; GD 116; Chancery; divorce

attorney for defendant; 1870 Jan; pg 147; GD 148; Law; debt $1000, damages $5000

attorney for plaintiff; 1870 Jan; pg 150; GD 163; Law; attachment

attorney for plaintiff; 1870 Jan; pg 152; GD 167; Law; attachment

attorney for defendant; 1870 Jan; pg 153; GD 168; Law; appeal

attorney for defendant; 1870 Jan; pg 153; GD 169; Law; mechanics lien

attorney for defendant; 1870 Jan; pg 154; GD 171; Law; mechanics lien

attorney for defendant; 1870 Jan; pg 154; [GD 170]; Law; attachment

attorney for defendant; 1870 Jan; pg 155; GD 172; Law; attachment

attorney for defendant; 1870 Jan; pg 155; GD 173; Law; attachment

attorney for defendant; 1870 Jan; pg 156; GD 175; Law; mechanics lien

attorney for defendant; 1870 Jan; pg 156; GD 174; Law; mechanics lien

attorney for defendant; 1870 Jan; pg 157; GD 177; Law; mechanics lien

attorney for defendant; 1870 Jan; pg 157; GD 176; Law; attachment

attorney for defendant; 1870 Jan; pg 158; GD 178; Law; attachment

attorney for plaintiff; 1870 Jan; pg 159; GD 180; Law; appeal

attorney for plaintiff; 1870 Jan; pg 161; GD 185; Law; assumpsit, damages $1000

attorney for defendant; 1870 Jan; pg 161; GD 184; Law; mechanics lien attorney for defendant; 1872 Jan; pg 261; GD 301; Law; mechanics lien

Wright & Berkley

attorney for plaintiff; 1868 July; pg 85; GD 71; Law; trespass

attorney for defendant; 1868 July; pg 86; GD 75; Law; appellant

attorney for defendant; 1868 July; pg 86; GD 76; Law; appellant

attorney for defendant; 1869 Jan; pg 108; GD 98; [Law]; trespass, $5000 damages

attorney for plaintiff; 1871 Jan; pg 193; GD 217; Law; appeal

Wright & Decker

attorney for defendant; 1868 July; pg 82; GD 36; Law; assumpsit

attorney for plaintiff; 1868 July; pg 85; GD 70; Law; assumpsit

attorney for plaintiff; 1868 July; pg 90; GD 91; Law; attachment

attorney for plaintiff; 1869 Jan; pg 106; GD 91; [Law]; attachment

attorney for defendant; 1869 Jan; pg 109; GD 118; [Law]; debt $1000, damages $5000

Wright & Trowbridge

attorney for plaintiff; 1872 Jan; pg 251; GD 263; Law; trespass, damages $2000

attorney for plaintiff; 1872 Jan; pg 251; GD 266; Law; unlawful forcible entry & detainer

Wright (A Wright & Company)

defendant; 1870 Jan; pg 153; GD 169; Law; mechanics lien

defendant; 1870 Jan; pg 154; GD 171; Law; mechanics lien

defendant; 1870 Jan; pg 154; [GD 170]; Law; attachment

defendant; 1870 Jan; pg 155; GD 173; Law; attachment

defendant; 1870 Jan; pg 155; GD 172; Law; attachment

defendant; 1870 Jan; pg 156; GD 174; Law; mechanics lien

defendant; 1870 Jan; pg 156; GD 175; Law; mechanics lien

defendant; 1870 Jan; pg 157; GD 177; Law; mechanics lien

defendant; 1870 Jan; pg 157; GD 176; Law; attachment

defendant; 1870 Jan; pg 158; GD 178; Law; attachment

defendant; 1870 Jan; pg 161; GD 184; Law; mechanics lien

defendant; 1871 Jan; pg 182; GD 169; Law; mechanics lien

defendant; 1871 Jan; pg 182; GD 170; Law; attachment

defendant; 1871 Jan; pg 183; GD 171; Law; mechanics lien

defendant; 1871 Jan; pg 183; GD 172; Law; attachment

defendant; 1871 Jan; pg 184; GD 174; Law; mechanics lien

defendant; 1871 Jan; pg 184; GD 173; Law; attachment

defendant; 1871 Jan; pg 185; GD 176; Law; attachment

defendant; 1871 Jan; pg 185; GD 175; Law; mechanics lien

defendant; 1871 Jan; pg 186; GD 177; Law; mechanics lien

defendant; 1871 Jan; pg 186; GD 178; Law; attachment

Wright (A Wright & Company), cont.

defendant; 1871 Jan; pg 188; GD 201; Law; attachment

defendant; 1871 Jan; pg 189; GD 203; Law; trespass on the case of premesis, damages $8000, attachment

plaintiff; 1871 Jan; pg 189; GD 202; Law; attachment

defendant; 1871 June; pg 222; GD 177; Law; mechanics lien

defendant; 1871 June; pg 222; GD 175; Law; mechanics lien

defendant; 1871 June; pg 223; GD 169; Law; mechanics lien

defendant; 1871 June; pg 223; GD 184; Law; mechanics lien

defendant; 1871 June; pg 224; GD 174; Law; mechanics lien

defendant; 1871 June; pg 224; GD 171; Law; mechanics lien

Wright (Berkley & Wright)

attorney for defendant; 1868 Mar; pg 68; GD 58; Law; assumpsit

attorney for plaintiff; 1868 Mar; pg 70; GD 71; Law; trespass

attorney for defendant; 1869 July; pg 116; GD 110; Criminal; murder

Wright (Browne, Decker & Wright)

attorney for defendant; 1870 Jan; pg 162; GD 158; Chancery

Wright (Decker & Wright)

attorney for defendant; 1867 Nov; pg 52; GD 57; Law; appeal

attorney for defendant; 1867 Nov; pg 54; Law; appeal

attorney for defendant; 1868 July; pg 91; GD 92; Law; trespass

Wright, A

attorney for plaintiff; [1872 Jan]; pg 319; GD 60; Law; mechanics lien

attorney for plaintiff; [1872 Jan]; pg 319; GD 145; Law; appeal

attorney for plaintiff; 1868 July; pg 84; GD 60; Law; mechanic lien

attorney for plaintiff; 1868 July; pg 98; GD 105; Chancery; divorce

attorney for plaintiff; 1868 July; pg 99; GD 106; Law [Chancery]; divorce

attorney for plaintiff; 1869 Jan; pg 105; GD 46; [Law]; mechanics lien

attorney for defendant; 1870 Jan; pg 141; GD 154; Criminal; indictment for larceny

attorney for defendant; 1870 Jan; pg 143; GD 126; Law; mechanics lien

attorney for defendant; 1870 Jan; pg 143; GD 125; Law; mechanics lien

attorney for defendant; 1870 Jan; pg 146; GD 141; Law; assumpsit, damages $2000

attorney for plaintiff; 1870 Jan; pg 146; GD 145; Law; appeal

attorney for defendant; 1870 Jan; pg 148; GD 152; Law; mechanics lien

attorney for plaintiff; 1870 Jan; pg 149; GD 161; Law; attachment

attorney for plaintiff; 1870 Jan; pg 150; GD 162; Law; attachment attorney for defendant; 1870 Jan; pg 166; Criminal; keeping open tippling house on Sabbath day

attorney for defendant; 1871 Jan; pg 196; GD 225; Law; appeal

attorney for defendant; 1871 Jan; pg 197; GD 226; Law; assumpsit

attorney for plaintiff; 1871 Jan; pg 198; GD 228; Law; attachment

attorney for plaintiff; 1871 Jan; pg 201; GD 208; Chancery; divorce

attorney for defendant; 1871 Jan; pg 205; GD 233; Law; appeal

attorney for defendant; 1871 June; pg 217; GD 254; Law

attorney for defendant; 1871 June; pg 218; GD 128; Law; mechanics lien

attorney for defendant; 1871 June; pg 218; GD 126; Law; mechanics lien

attorney for defendant; 1871 June; pg 219; GD 126; Law; mechanics lien

attorney for defendant; 1871 June; pg 219; GD 150; Law; mechanics lien

attorney for plaintiff; 1871 June; pg 227; GD 263; Law; trespass, damages $2000

attorney for plaintiff; 1871 June; pg 228; GD 266; Law; willful forcible entry & detainer

attorney for plaintiff; 1871 June; pg 230; GD 275; Law; assumpsit

attorney for defendant; 1871 June; pg 233; GD 158; Chancery; divorce

attorney for plaintiff; 1871 June; pg 234; GD 257; Chancery; divorce

attorney for defendant; 1872 Jan; pg 246; GD 150; Law; mechanics lien

attorney for defendant; 1872 Jan; pg 246; GD 125; Law; mechanics lien

attorney for defendant; 1872 Jan; pg 255; GD 282; Law; appeal

attorney for plaintiff; 1872 Jan; pg 257; GD 292; Law; trespass, damage $5000

attorney for plaintiff; 1872 Jan; pg 258; GD 294; Law; appeal

attorney for plaintiff; 1872 Jan; pg 260; GD 298; Law; assumpsit, damages $300

attorney for plaintiff; 1872 Jan; pg 262; GD 301; Law; replevin

attorney for plaintiff; 1872 Jan; pg 265; GD 291; Chancery; writ of injunction

attorney for plaintiff; 1872 Jan; pg 266; GD 276; Chancery; Petition of Mary M Humphries, widow &c to sell real estate

attorney for plaintiff; 1872 Jan; pg 266; GD 285; Chancery; bill for foreclosure of mortgage

attorney for defendant; 1872 Jan; pg 267; GD 255; Chancery; divorce

attorney for plaintiff; 1872 Jan; pg 267; GD 283; Chancery; divorce

attorney for plaintiff; 1872 Jan; pg 268; GD 286; Chancery; divorce

attorney for plaintiff; 1872 Jan; pg 269; GD 305; Chancery; demands

Wright, Alpheus

defendant; [1868 July]; pg 93; GD 97; Law; trespass

defendant; [1868 July]; pg 93; GD 96; Law; trespass

defendant; 1868 July; pg 92; GD 95; Law; trespass

defendant; 1868 July; pg 94; GD 99; Law; trespass

defendant; 1868 July; pg 94; GD 98; Law; trespass

defendant; 1868 July; pg 95; GD 100; Law; trespass

defendant; 1868 July; pg 95; GD 101; Law; trespass

defendant; 1868 July; pg 96; GD 102; Law; trespass

defendant; 1868 July; pg 96; GD 103; Law; [trespass]

defendant; 1868 July; pg 97; GD 104; Law; trespass

defendant; 1868 Mar; pg 75; GD 82; Law; effectment

defendant; 1868 Mar; pg 75; GD 81; Law; trespass

defendant; 1868 Mar; pg 87; GD 78; Law; trespass

defendant; 1868 Mar; pg 87; GD 79; Law; trespass

defendant; 1868 Mar; pg 88; GD 81; Law; trespass

defendant; 1868 Mar; pg 88; GD 80; Law; trespass

defendant; 1869 Jan; pg 105; GD 78; [Law]; trespass, $5000 damages

defendant; 1869 Jan; pg 106; GD 81; [Law]; trespass, $1000 damages

defendant; 1869 Jan; pg 108; GD 98; [Law]; trespass, $5000 damages

defendant; 1869 July; pg 117; GD 78; Law; trespass, $5000 damages

defendant; 1869 July; pg 118; GD 99; Law; trespass, $5000 damages

defendant; 1869 July; pg 118; GD 81; Law; trespass, $10,000 damages

defendant; 1869 July; pg 129; GD 147; Law; assumpsit, Damages $500

defendant; 1870 Jan; pg 151; GD 165; Law; attachment

defendant; 1870 Jan; pg 153; GD 169; Law; mechanics lien

defendant; 1870 Jan; pg 154; GD 171; Law; mechanics lien

defendant; 1870 Jan; pg 154; [GD 170]; Law; attachment

defendant; 1870 Jan; pg 155; GD 172; Law; attachment

defendant; 1870 Jan; pg 155; GD 173; Law; attachment

defendant; 1870 Jan; pg 156; GD 174; Law; mechanics lien

defendant; 1870 Jan; pg 156; GD 175; Law; mechanics lien

defendant; 1870 Jan; pg 157; GD 176; Law; attachment

defendant; 1870 Jan; pg 157; GD 177; Law; mechanics lien

defendant; 1870 Jan; pg 158; GD 178; Law; attachment

defendant; 1870 Jan; pg 161; GD 184; Law; mechanics lien

Z

Additional Colorado Research Titles

If you borrowed this copy from a library and would like to order a copy, please send a check or money order to: Iron Gate Publishing, P.O. Box 999, Niwot, CO 80544. Our research books are available online to institutions and individuals at Amazon.com and on our website:

www.irongate.com

Boulder County District Court Judge's Docket, Vol 1, 1867-1871: An Annotated Index
ISBN 978-1-68224-026-7 $15.95 + $4.00 S&H

Boulder County, Colorado District Court Record, June 1862 to March 1866: An Annotated Transcription
ISBN 978-1-68224-024-3, $11.95 + $4.00 S&H

Boulder County, Colorado Treasurer, Register of Accounts, 1867-1880: An Annotated Index
ISBN 978-1-68224-023-6, $19.95 + $5.00 S&H

Inventors in the Colorado Territory and their U.S. Patents, 1861-1876: An Annotated Index
ISBN 978-1-68224-022-9 $54.95 + $5.00 S&H

Boulder County, Colorado County Court Index Book I, Plaintiffs and Defendants: An Annotated Index
ISBN 978-1-68224-021-2 $34.95 + $5.00

Minutes of the Board of Trustees of the University of Colorado, 1870-1876: An Annotated Index
ISBN 978-1-68224-020-5 $11.95 + $4.00 S&H

Boulder County, Colorado District Court Civil Appearance Docket, 1878-1882: An Annotated Index
ISBN 978-1-68224-019-9 $19.95 + $5.00 S&H

Boulder County, Colorado County Court Will Record, Volume A, 1875-1889: An Annotated Index
ISBN 978-1-68224-018-2 $11.95 + $4.00 S&H

Boulder County, Colorado, County Court Probate Record, Vol 1, 1875-1884: An Annotated Index
ISBN 978-1-68224-017-5 $11.95 + $4.00 S&H

Early Land Owners Along the St. Vrain Creek, Colorado Territory, 1860-1861: An Annotated Index
ISBN 978-1-68224-006-9 $11.95 + $4.00 S&H

Boulder County, Colorado District Court Widow's Relinquishment, Volumes 1 & 2, 1889–1937: An Annotated Index
ISBN 978-1-68224-009-0 $11.95 + $4.00 S&H

Boulder County, Colorado, District Court Guardians Bonds, Vol. A, 1876-1902: An Annotated Index
ISBN 978-1-879579-78-1 $11.95 + $4.00 S&H

Boulder County, Colorado Probate Court Fee Book, 1874-1890: An Annotated Index
ISBN 978-1-879579-88-0 $11.95 + $4.00 S&H

Boulder City Town Company Lot Sales 1859-1864: An Annotated Map Guide
ISBN 978-1-879579-87-3 $15.95 + $5.00 S&H

Brainard's Hotel Register, Boulder, Colorado, 1880: An Annotated Index
ISBN 978-1-879579-86-6 $15.95 $5.00 S&H

Boulder County Commissioner's Journal, 1861-1871: An Annotated Transcription
ISBN 978-1-879579-77-4 $45.99 + $5.00 S&H

Boulder County Commissioners Journal, 1871-1874: An Annotated Transcription
ISBN 978-1-879579-91-0 $39.95 + $5.00 S&H

Colorado's Territorial Masons: An Annotated Index of the Proceedings of the Grand Lodge of Colorado, 1861–1876
ISBN 978-1-879579-85-9 $29.95 + $5.00 S&H

Boulder, Colorado Teachers, 1878-1900: An Annotated Index
ISBN 978-1-879579-93-4 $11.95 + $4.00 S&H

Boulder County, Colorado District Court Execution Docket, 1875-1885: An Annotated Index
ISBN 978-1-879579-94-1 $11.95 + $4.00 S&H

Denver, Colorado Police Force Record, 1879-1903: An Annotated Index
ISBN 978-1-879579-81-1 $11.95 + $4.00 S&H

Boulder, Colorado Births 1892–1906: An Annotated Index
ISBN 978-1-879579-79-8 $11.95 + $4.00 S&H

Arapahoe County, Colorado Territory Criminal Court Index, 1862-1879: An Annotated Index
ISBN 978-1-879579-70-5 $11.95 + $4.00 S&H

Boulder County Probate Court Appraisement Record A, 1875-1888: An Annotated Index
ISBN 978-1-879579-72-9 $11.95 + $4.00 S&H

Boulder County Assessor's Tax List, 1875: An Annotated Index
ISBN 978-1-879579-55-2 $11.95 + $4.00 S&H

Boulder County Assessor's Tax List, 1876: An Annotated Index
ISBN 978-1-879579-56-9 $11.95 + $4.00 S&H

Boulder Valley Presbyterian Church Records, 1863-1900: An Annotated Index
ISBN 978-1-879579-58-3 $11.95 + $4.00 S&H

Boulder's Masonic Pioneers, 1867-1886: Members of Columbia Lodge No. 14, Boulder County, Colorado Territory
ISBN 978-1-879579-57-6 $15.95 + $4.00 S&H

Map: Boulder City Town Company 1859 Original Survey Map
ISBN 978-1-68224-000-7 $24.95 (PAPER) + $7.00 S&H
ISBN 978-1-68224-001-4 $74.95 (MYLAR) + $7.00 S&H

Map: Boulder City Town Company, 11 Aug 1859 Land Lottery Map Showing Lot Purchases
ISBN 978-1-68224-002-1 $24.95 (PAPER) + $7.00 S&H
ISBN 978-1-68224-003-8 $74.95 (MYLAR) + $7.00 S&H

Map: Boulder City Town Company 20 Sept 1859 Map Showing Stock Certificates Issued by Lot
ISBN 978-1-68224-004-5 $24.95 (PAPER) + $7.00 S&H
ISBN 978-1-68224-005-2 $74.95 (MYLAR) + $7.00 S&H

Publishing Titles

If you would like to order one of these books, please send a check or money order to: Iron Gate Publishing, P.O. Box 999, Niwot, CO 80544. Our books are available online to institutions through Ingram, to individuals at Amazon.com and on our website:

www.irongate.com

Set Yourself Up to Self-Publish: A Genealogist's Guide
     ISBN 978-1-879579-99-6 $19.95 + $5.00 S&H

Set Yourself Up to Self-Publish: A Local Historian's Guide
     ISBN 978-1-879579-98-9 $19.95 + $5.00

Publish Your Genealogy: A Step-by-Step Guide for Preserving Your Research for the Next Generation
     ISBN 978-1-879579-62-0 $24.95 + $5.00 S&H

Publish Your Family History: A Step-by-Step Guide to Writing the Stories of Your Ancestors
     ISBN 978-1-879579-63-7 $24.95 + $5.00 S&H

Publish a Local History: A Step-by-Step Guide from Finding the Right Project to Finished Book
     ISBN 978-1-879579-64-4 $24.95 + $5.00 S&H

Publish a Memoir: A Step-by-Step Guide to Saving Your Memories for Future Generations
     ISBN 978-1-879579-65-1 $24.95 + $5.00 S&H

Publish a Biography: A Step-by-Step Guide to Capturing the Life and Times of an Ancestor or a Generation
     ISBN 978-1-879579-66-8 $24.95 + $5.00 S&H

Publish a Photo Book: A Step-by-Step Guide for Transforming Your Genealogical Research into a Stunning Family Heirloom
     ISBN 978-1-879579-67-5 $24.95 + $5.00 S&H

Publish a Source Index: A Step-by-Step Guide to Creating a Genealogically Useful Index, Abstract or Transcription
     ISBN 978-1-879579-68-2 $24.95 + $5.00 S&H

Publish Your Specialty: A Step-by-Step Guide for Imparting Your Research Expertise to Others
     ISBN 978-1-879579-76-7 $24.95 + $5.00 S&H